Teen Finance Series

FINANCIAL LITERACY INFORMATION FOR TEENS FIRST EDITION

Teen Finance Series

FINANCIAL LITERACY INFORMATION FOR TEENS FIRST EDITION

Tips for a Successful Financial Life

Including Facts about Earning Money, Budgeting, Savings and Investments, Banking, Credit Unions, Credit Cards, Debt, and Latest Trends in Financial Technology

OMNIGRAPHICS
An imprint of Infobase

* * *

OMNIGRAPHICS
An imprint of Infobase
8 The Green, Suite #19225
Dover, DE 19901

www.infobase.com

James Chambers, *Managing Editor*

* * *

ISBN 978-0-7808-1966-5
E-ISBN 978-0-7808-1967-2

Library of Congress Cataloging-in-Publication Data

Names: Hayes, Kevin (Writer on finance) editor.

Title: Financial literacy information for teens / edited by Kevin Hayes.

Description: First Edition. | Detroit, MI: Omnigraphics, Inc., 2021. | Series: Teen finance series | Includes index. | Audience: Ages 13 | Audience: Grades 7-9 | Summary: "Provides tips for financial success including facts about earning money, creating budget, savings and investments, banking, credit unions, credit cards, debt and financial technology along with a list of apps available for various financial processes and resources for additional information"-- Provided by publisher.

Identifiers: LCCN 2021032516 (print) | LCCN 2021032517 (ebook) | ISBN 9780780819665 (library binding) | ISBN 9780780819672 (ebook)

Subjects: LCSH: Finance, Personal--Juvenile literature. | Financial literacy.

Classification: LCC HG173.8 .F56 2021 (print) | LCC HG173.8 (ebook) | DDC 332.024--dc23

LC record available at https://lccn.loc.gov/2021032516
LC ebook record available at https://lccn.loc.gov/2021032517

This book is printed on acid-free paper meeting the ANSI Z39.48 Standard. The infinity symbol that appears above indicates that the paper in this book meets that standard.

Printed in the United States

TABLE OF CONTENTS

Part 3 | Financial Fundamentals

Part 4 | Credit Cards and Credit Scores

Part 5 | Staying Out of Debt

Part 6 | Financial Apps and Data Security Concerns

Part 7 | If You Need More Help or Information

PREFACE

About This Book

Today's teens are spending their own money, and they are spending a lot of it. But, the challenges that come with managing and spending that money have never been more daunting. Faced with greater personal responsibility for managing their own money, and changing technology that has created both opportunity and risk, today's teens face economic challenges unlike any previous generation. Unfortunately, many teens are lacking the basic financial literacy needed to meet those challenges. As a result, the majority of today's teens remain unaware of basic financial principles, such as earning, budgeting, saving, establishing credit, and managing debt. In addition, many teens are unaware of the risks that come with the technology that while making their lives easier, also makes their personal and financial information more vulnerable than ever before.

Financial Literacy Information for Teens, First Edition outlines the principles of earning, spending, and managing money. It provides information about financial goals and budgeting. It highlights the importance of saving and investing money and also talks about the risks involved in investing. The basics of banking are discussed along with the details about savings and checking accounts. The benefits and risks of electronic banking, online fund transfer, mobile wallets are also discussed. It discusses the importance of credit history and explains how to choose and manage a credit card. It talks about the various loan options available for people under 18 years of age and also the problems associated with debt. It provides information about the latest trends in financial technology and lists several tools and apps available for various financial processes. The book concludes with a directory of resources for additional information.

How to Use This Book

This book is divided into parts and chapters. Parts focus on broad areas of interest; chapters are devoted to single topics within a part.

Part 1: Earning Money and Creating a Budget begins by outlining the principles of managing money and explains how to set financial goals. It continues with information about career planning and common ways teens can acquire money. Information about budgeting and smart spending is also included.

Part 2: Saving and Investing Strategies provides a roadmap to saving and investing. It describes banking basics, and offers information on how to set up a savings account. It also offers suggestions on how to invest and grow your money. A chapter on the risks involved in investing is also provided.

Part 3: Financial Fundamentals explains how to read an invoice and a bank statement. Details about checking accounts and how to manage a checking account are provided. The benefits and risks of electronic banking, online fund transfer, and mobile wallets are also discussed.

Part 4: Credit Cards and Credit Scores explains how credit works and the importance of building a good credit history. It provides information on choosing and managing a credit card. Problems resulting from making minimum payments with high-interest rates are discussed.

Part 5: Staying Out of Debt talks about the various loan options available for people under 18 years of age. The problems associated with debt are highlighted along with the information on how to deal with debt.

Part 6: Financial Apps and Data Security Concerns talks about the latest technologies that aim at enhancing financial services. The tools and apps available for various financial processes such as budgeting, paying bills, tracking money, etc. are discussed. It also provides information on protecting financial information.

Part 7: If You Need More Help or Information includes a directory of resources for additional information about personal finance.

Bibliographic Note

This volume contains documents and excerpts from publications issued by the following U.S. government agencies: AmeriCorps; Consumer Financial Protection Bureau (CFPB); Federal Communications Commission (FCC); Federal Deposit Insurance Corporation (FDIC); Federal Student Aid; Federal Trade Commission (FTC); Inverstor.gov; MyCreditUnion.gov; MyMoney.gov; Small Business Administration (SBA); U.S. Bureau of Labor Statistics (BLS); U.S. Department of Labor (DOL); U.S. Securities and Exchange Commission (SEC); and Youth.gov.

It also contains original material produced by Omnigraphics.

PART 1 | EARNING MONEY AND CREATING A BUDGET

CHAPTER 1

THE FIVE PRINCIPLES OF MANAGING AND GROWING MONEY

About This Chapter: This chapter includes text excerpted from "My Money Five," MyMoney.gov, Financial Literacy and Education Commission (FLEC), May 31, 2013.

My Money Five

Making the most of your money starts with five building blocks for managing and growing your money – The MyMoney Five. Keep these five principles in mind as you make day-to-day decisions and plan your financial goals.

Earn

The Earn principle is about more than the amount you are paid through work. This principle is about knowing the fine print and details about your paycheck, including deductions and withholdings. To put it another way: In order to make the most of what you earn, it helps to understand your pay and benefits.

Actions You Can Take

- Learn about the details of your paycheck, including any deductions.
- Review the taxes that are withheld, including Social Security and Medicare taxes.
- Explore and sign up for workplace benefits.
- Invest in your future – with education and training.

Hints and Tips

- Remember, your employer has to subtract certain taxes and other items from your wages every pay period. Your take-home pay (net income) is what you receive after any taxes and deductions are subtracted.
- Usually, your deductions and withholdings include federal, state and city income taxes, Social Security and Medicare taxes, your contributions for

retirement savings, and payments for health insurance provided as part of your job.

- Be sure you take advantage of all the credits and deductions that help lower your taxes.
- It is a good idea to sign up if your employer offers a retirement savings program. If so, you can arrange to have retirement savings automatically moved from your paycheck to a retirement account. Many employers will match part of every dollar you save this way, and you will benefit from it when you retire.

Save and Invest

Saving is a key principle. People who make a habit of saving regularly, even saving small amounts, are well on their way to success. It is important to open a bank or credit union account so it will be simple and easy for you to save regularly. Then, use your savings to plan for life events and to be ready for unplanned or emergency needs.

Actions You Can Take

- Start saving, form a savings habit, and pay yourself first!
- Open and keep an account at a bank or credit union that meets your needs.
- Track your savings and investments, and monitor what you own.
- Plan for short-term and long-term goals.
- Build up emergency savings for unexpected events.
- Consult with a qualified professional on investments and other key financial matters.
- Save for retirement, children's education and other major items.

Hints and Tips

- An easy way to save is to pay yourself first. That means each pay period, before you are tempted to spend money, commit to putting some in a savings account. See if you can arrange with your bank to automatically transfer a certain amount from your paycheck or your checking account to savings every month.
- People who keep track of their savings often end up saving more, because they have it on their minds. New phone apps are available to help people pass up purchases they do not really need – you might want to try one!
- If you are making investments, it is good to consult with a qualified professional about your plans. Before you purchase investments, be sure to build an emergency savings fund to cover your needs for at least three months. Keep the savings in an insured bank or credit union account that you can access if you need it.

- Many professionals call themselves "financial planners." Before you hire one, ask for a description of the services offered. A good place to check the credentials of an investment advisor is your state's consumer protection office, the state's Attorney General's office, or the issuing agency for any professional licenses or certifications.

> Financial education and hands-on savings account experience at an early age can increase opportunities for financial success.
> *(Source: "Going to College," MyCreditUnion.gov.)*

Protect

The Protect principle means taking precautions about your financial situation. It stresses the importance of accumulating savings in case of an emergency, and buying insurance. Be vigilant about identity theft, and keep aware of your credit record and the credit score.

Actions You Can Take

- Keep your financial records in order.
- Watch out for fraud and scams, and protect your identity.
- Choose insurance to meet your needs, including healthcare insurance.

Hints and Tips

- A good system for keeping personal money records will include copies of important documents such as your will, property ownership documents, information about savings and insurance, and other document. It should include overview of what happens to property after a major life event occurs.
- Assume that any offer that "sounds too good to be true" – especially one from a stranger or an unfamiliar company – is probably a fraud.
- Look at your bank statements and bills as soon as they arrive and report any discrepancy or anything suspicious, such as an unauthorized withdrawal or charge.
- Be wary of request to "update" or "confirm" personal information, especially your Social Security number, bank account numbers, credit card numbers, personal identification numbers, your date of birth or your mother's maiden name in response to an unsolicited call, letter, or e-mail.

Spend

The fundamental concept of Spend is: Make a budget or a plan for using your money wisely. It is helpful to set short- and long-term financial goals and manage your money to meet them.

Actions You Can Take

- Live within your means.
- Be a smart shopper, and compare prices and quality.
- Track your spending habits and develop a budget or spending plan.
- Plan for short-term and long-term financial goals.

Hints and Tips

- A good way to take control of your spending is to set the maximum amounts you plan to spend each week or each month. Once you have set the maximum, stick with your plan.
- It is helpful to track your spending over a few weeks or months to get a handle on how you are using your dollars and cents. Look into using online systems or phone apps for keeping track of your spending – you will be amazed at what you will learn about your habits!
- Be careful not to let a sale or discount coupon persuade you to purchase something you do not really need and that is not in your spending plan.
- When planning a big purchase, take time to comparison shop and check prices at a few different stores, by phone or online.

Borrow

Sometimes it is necessary to Borrow for major purchases such as an education, a car, a house, or maybe even to meet unexpected expenses. Your ability to get a loan generally depends on your credit history, and that depends largely on your track record at repaying what you have borrowed in the past and paying your bills on time. So, be careful to keep your credit history strong.

Actions You Can Take

- Track your borrowing habits.
- Pay your bills on time.
- When you need to borrow, be sure to plan, understand and shop around for a loan with a low annual percentage rate (APR).
- Learn about credit and how to use it effectively.
- Pay attention to your credit history, as reflected by your credit score and on your credit report.

Hints and Tips

- Borrowing money is a way to purchase something now and pay for it over time. But, you usually pay "interest" when you borrow money. The longer you take to pay back the money you borrowed, the more you will pay in interest.
- It pays to shop around to get the best deal on a loan. Compare loan terms from several lenders, and it is okay to negotiate the terms.

- When repaying a loan, it may be better to pay more than the minimum amount due each month, so you will have to pay less in interest over the life of the loan.
- One of your most important aids when shopping for a loan is the APR – the annual percentage rate. This is the total cost, including interest charges and fees, described as a yearly rate.
- Paying your bills on time will help increase your credit score. Even if you fell into trouble with borrowing in the past, you can get on solid footing and rebuild your credit history by making regular payments as agreed.
- You are entitled to a free copy of your credit report every 12 months from each of the three nationwide credit bureaus. Go to www.AnnualCreditReport.com or call toll free 877-322-8228 to order the free reports. Beware of imposter sites.

CHAPTER 2

BUILDING BLOCKS OF FINANCIAL CAPABILITY

About This Chapter: This chapter includes text excerpted from "Learn about the Building Blocks of Financial Capability," Consumer Financial Protection Bureau (CFPB), October 23, 2018.

Findings from CFPB's research suggest that the knowledge, skills, and behaviors associated with adult financial capability stem from three interconnected building blocks developed in youth. These building blocks form a framework for youth financial literacy education. Children and youth need all three of the interconnected building blocks to achieve financial capability.

Financial education is a strategy that provides people with financial knowledge, skills, and resources so they can get, manage, and use their money to achieve their goals. Financial education builds an individual's knowledge, skills, and capacity to use resources and tools, including financial products and services. Financial education leads to financial literacy.

(Source: "A Financial Empowerment Toolkit for Community Volunteers," Consumer Financial Protection Bureau (CFPB).)

Executive Function

Executive function skills help people stay focused and manage the flow of information. Day-to-day, these skills allow a person to pay attention, plan ahead, remember details, and juggle multiple tasks. They also help control their behavior and emotions, delay immediate rewards for future benefits, and continue forward when faced with challenges.

Building Executive Function

Teaching young children how to have self-control and think before they act lays the groundwork for good financial skills in the future.

Table 2.1. Early Childhood (Ages 3–5)

Milestones for Executive Function	What It May Look like in Adulthood
Begins to control their own behaviors and emotions	Thinks twice before buying, avoids making emotional purchases, avoids financial temptations
Begins to stay focused and complete tasks	Follows a budget, sticks to a shopping list
Shows the above skills when using and managing limited resources such as time, money, treats, or belongings	Spends within their means, uses coupons and sales to reduce spending

Table 2.2. Middle Childhood (Ages 6–12)

Milestones for Executive Function	What It May Look like in Adulthood
Delays immediate reward for future benefit	Saves money now for an item they want later
Begins to think about how current actions may lead to future results	Puts money in the bank to earn interest and increase future savings

Importance of Executive Function

People need the skills associated with executive function to do things such as set financial goals, decide when to buy and when to save, and make and follow a budget – all of which contribute to adult financial well-being.

Development of This Building Block

Most people start to develop basic executive functions during early childhood. The skills acquired during this time lay a foundation for the more complex aspects of executive function that develop throughout middle childhood and into early adulthood.

The tables that follow show what this building block looks like at three stages of development and how the skills and abilities relate to adult behavior associated with financial well-being.

Teaching This Building Block

An effective way to build executive function is to use a combination of teaching strategies and learning activities that allow students to practice these skills frequently in a variety of situations across content areas.

Instructional Strategies

Research shows that the following are among the instructional strategies that can help students develop executive function:

- **Cooperative learning.** Small groups of students work together to build their knowledge and understanding of a subject while developing positive relationships and the ability to work as a team.

Table 2.3. Adolescence and Young Adulthood (Ages 13–21)

Milestones for Executive Function	What It May Look like in Adulthood
Demonstrates critical thinking skills, such as researching, analyzing, and comparing information	Compares features and costs on big purchases, knows where to find credible financial information, searches for sales and deals
Thinks about the long term and believes there will be opportunities in the future	Plans for retirement, explores ways to increase income
Shows the ability to plan, set goals, and delay immediate reward for future gain	Sets aside regular savings toward future purchases, contributes to retirement account
Knows how to start an activity or project	Creates a financial plan for purchasing a car or home
Controls impulses and thinks creatively to address unexpected challenges	Spends to meet needs before wants, adjusts spending after loss of income or addition of new expenses, learns from financial mistakes
Remembers key information	Weighs financial decisions based on their own and others' past experiences

- **Personalized instruction.** Teacher tailors instruction to the individual student, including focusing resources, strategies, supports, and pacing on that student's needs.
- **Simulation.** Hands-on learning activities that use real-world scenarios to promote critical thinking and applied learning.

Learning Activities

Learning activities that nurture executive function should stimulate working memory, cognitive flexibility, self-regulation, self-management, persistence, and focus. The types of activities that support these skills include the following:

- **Intergenerational programs.** Intentional dual generational collaborations between adults (parents, volunteers, senior citizens, etc.) and young people that promote learning and growth and allow older adults to mentor youth and/or share their knowledge and experiences in meaningful ways.
- **Planning activities.** Exercises that support students in creating and following a plan to complete a task or accomplish a goal.
- **Pretend play.** Make-believe plays where children use their imaginations to act out stories and take on new roles and personas.
- **Puzzles and quiet games.** Opportunities to engage and challenge students through problem-solving tasks that help them learn and apply new skills, understand complex concepts, and develop vocabulary.
- **Self-directed exploration.** Active learning experiences that give students choices and allow them to explore and discover new topics, ideas, and skills based on their interests and readiness.

- **Storytelling.** The act of telling a story orally, while using different voices, dramatic inflections, or other narrative embellishments.

Financial Habits and Norms

Financial habits and norms are the values, standards, routine practices, and rules to live by that people rely on to navigate their day-to-day financial lives. They support the ability to effectively manage money and respond quickly to financial decisions or challenges.

Importance of Financial Habits and Norms

The skills associated with financial habits and norms allow a person to more easily make financial decisions based on their attitudes, values, emotions, social norms, and contextual cues. These skills help a person decide what is desirable and possible financially and guide their day-to-day behaviors. This could range from decisions about splurging on a treat to how much to save in a retirement account.

Development of This Building Block

People typically begin to build money habits, norms, and values during middle childhood through a process called "financial socialization." These habits and norms continue to develop through adolescence and influence many financial behaviors and habits in adulthood.

The tables that follow show what this building block looks like at three stages of development and how the skills and abilities relate to adult behavior associated with financial well-being.

Teaching This Building Block

School is one of many places where financial socialization occurs. Across the curriculum, classroom activities can help students practice financial behaviors and begin to develop a sense of their own money management preferences.

Instructional Strategies

Research shows that the following are among the instructional strategies that can help students develop financial habits and norms:

- **Blended learning.** When learning is structured to include both online and in-person experiences, which can promote personalized learning and flexible pacing
- **Gamification.** A highly motivating learning strategy that uses game elements, mechanics, and/or game-based thinking (as opposed to playing an entire game) and requires creativity and collaboration.
- **Simulation.** Hands-on learning activities that use real-world scenarios to promote critical thinking and application of learning.

Table 2.4. Early Childhood (Ages 3–5)

Milestones for Financial Habits and Norms	What It May Look like in Adulthood
Begins to develop basic values and attitudes around keeping (saving) and using (consuming) resources	Thinks twice before buying, saves money now for an item they want later

Table 2.5. Middle Childhood (Ages 6–12)

Milestones for Financial Habits and Norms	What It May Look like in Adulthood
Begins to develop a positive attitude toward planning, saving, frugality, and self-control	Plans and saves for big purchases, spends money on needs before wants, limits splurge purchases
Begins to show positive financial habits, such as planning and saving	Makes a financial plan (formal or informal), sets aside regular savings
Begins to make spending and saving decisions that match personal goals and values	Thinks about positive and negative effects of today's purchases on future financial goals
Feels confident about completing age-appropriate financial tasks, such as deciding how to spend allowance and depositing money in a savings account	Pays bills on time, understands options for saving and investing, trusts ability to make good financial decisions

Table 2.6. Adolescence and Early Adulthood (Ages 13–21)

Milestones for Financial Habits and Norms	What It May Look like in Adulthood
Demonstrates a positive attitude toward planning, saving, frugality, and self-control	Makes and follows a budget, saves for big purchases and for retirement
Shows positive money management habits and decision-making strategies	Lives within their means, compares features and costs to make an informed purchase
Makes spending and saving decisions that match personal goals and values; resists peer pressure	Measures financial success by own standards instead of others', spends with values and goals for today and the future in mind
Confidently completes age-appropriate financial tasks, such as getting a part-time job and using debit and credit cards	Makes a financial plan, explores employment options, limits credit card use, avoids and manages debt

Learning Activities

Learning activities that nurture financial habits and norms should promote healthy money habits, norms, rules to live by, and decision shortcuts for navigating day-to-day financial life and effective routine money management. The types of activities that support these skills include the following:

- **Employment opportunities.** Activities that provide a way for students to explore and prepare for job options and make clear connections between school and career
- **Entrepreneurship.** Opportunities for young people to create their own companies (real or imagined) and, in doing so, apply critical-thinking, innovation, communication, and collaboration skills
- **Financial simulations.** Educational tools or activities that replicate real-world financial management situations and allow students to develop skills such as budgeting, comparison shopping, and investing by making mock decisions that result in realistic consequences
- **Understanding financial products.** Activities that allow students to explore financial tools and products used to buy things, save, invest, get insurance, or get a mortgage

Financial Knowledge and Decision-Making Skills

Financial knowledge and decision-making skills help people make informed financial decisions through problem-solving, critical thinking, and an understanding of key financial facts and concepts.

Importance of Financial Knowledge and Decision-Making Skills

Strong financial knowledge and decision-making skills help people weigh options and make informed choices for their financial situations, such as deciding how and when to save and spend, comparing costs before a big purchase, and planning for retirement or other long-term savings.

Development of This Building Block

Financial knowledge and decision-making skills typically do not develop until adolescence and young adulthood. During these years, they become more relevant, especially for youth who start to earn money, buy things on their own, manage a bank account, or borrow for education.

The tables that follow show what this building block looks like at three stages of development and how the skills and abilities relate to adult behavior associated with financial well-being.

Teaching This Building Block

Schools can provide opportunities for youth to practice financial behaviors, make financial decisions, and reflect on the outcomes and consequences of those decisions. Across the curriculum, teachers can provide opportunities for students to learn how to find and recognize reliable financial information, compare financial products, and do purposeful financial research in order to analyze options and make decisions.

Table 2.7. Early Childhood (Ages 3–5)

Milestones for Financial Knowledge and Decision-Making Skills	What It May Look like in Adulthood
Has early math skills like counting and sorting	Calculates change owed at point of sale, categorizes spending for budgeting, tracks cash flow
Grasps very basic financial concepts like money and trading	Estimates costs, calculates discounts or sales tax

Table 2.8. Middle Childhood (Ages 6–12)

Milestones for Financial Knowledge and Decision-Making Skills	What It May Look like in Adulthood
Understands basic financial concepts	Has a realistic idea of how much things cost, saves a portion of earnings, pays bills on time, makes a budget
Successfully manages money (like their allowance) or other resources to reach personal goals	Spends to meet needs before wants, follows a budget, saves for big purchases or events (e.g., vacation)

Table 2.9. Adolescence and Early Adulthood (Ages 13–21)

Milestones for Financial Knowledge and Decision-Making Skills	What It May Look like in Adulthood
Understands advanced financial concepts and processes	Understands risks and benefits of investing, uses credit wisely, manages debt
Routinely manages money or other resources to reach personal goals	Spends with values and goals for today and the future in mind, pays day-to-day and month-to-month expenses, saves for retirement, has financial flexibility to splurge once in a while
Identifies trusted sources of financial information and accurately uses them to compare and make decisions	Seeks credible information (e.g., "Consumer Reports," product labels, store ads), compares features and costs before making big purchases, consults trusted advisers, knows the difference between a bargain and a scam

Instructional Strategies

Research shows that the following strategies can be effective to help people develop financial knowledge and decision-making skills:

- **Competency-based learning.** Student-centered learning that encourages students to progress toward well-defined benchmarks to give them a sense of mastery and ownership over the skills and knowledge they are learning
- **Direct instruction.** A structured, straightforward, teacher-directed approach that focuses on an explicit skill and typically includes a lecture, demonstration, or discussion

- **Personalized instruction.** Teacher assesses each student's needs, then tailors instruction to the individual student, including focusing and differentiating resources, strategies, supports, and pacing on that student's needs to individualize learning
- **Project-based learning.** A hands-on strategy in which students actively explore real-world challenges, answer meaningful questions, and accomplish relevant tasks and, in doing so, are encouraged to make their own decisions, perform their own research, overcome obstacles, and present their work to others
- **Simulation.** Hands-on learning activities that use real-world scenarios to promote critical thinking and application of learning

Learning Activities

Learning activities that nurture financial knowledge and decision-making should support young people's acquisition of factual knowledge, research and analysis skills, and deliberate financial decision-making. The types of activities that support these skills include the following:

- **Financial coaching and mentoring.** Adults engage and encourage students (individually and in small groups) to develop financial capability and work toward financial goals.
- **Financial simulations.** Educational tools or activities that replicate real-world financial management situations and allow students to develop skills such as budgeting, comparison shopping, and investing by making mock decisions that result in realistic consequences.
- **Real-world case studies.** Stories that present realistic situations involving a dilemma, conflict, or problem to be negotiated or resolved by analyzing and evaluating a range of information and weighing the consequences of different decisions.

CHAPTER 3
FINANCIAL GOALS

About This Chapter: Text in this chapter begins with excerpts from "My SMART Goals," Federal Deposit Insurance Corporation (FDIC), April 9, 2021; Text under the heading "Stay Focused on Your Goals" is excerpted from "Stay Focused on My Goals," Federal Deposit Insurance Corporation (FDIC), April 9, 2021.

Setting goals helps you prioritize how you use your money, so it goes toward what matters to you. Setting goals can also help you measure and track your progress toward achieving your hopes and dreams.

Use the acronym SMART to remember that goals should be Specific, Measurable, Action-oriented, Reachable, and Time-bound.

Table 3.1. SMART Goals

To Ensure Your Goals Are...	Ask Yourself...
Specific	What exactly do you want to accomplish? Why is this important to you? Is this something you really want?
Measurable	How much? How many? How will you know when you have met your goal?
Action-oriented	What specific actions do you need to complete to meet this goal?
Reachable	Is this goal something you can actually reach?
Time-bound	When will you reach this goal?

Stay Focused on Your Goals

You can use these strategies to stay focused on your goals by blocking unproductive messages and resisting impulse spending. You may have other strategies that work for you.

Recognize the Tactics Used to Influence You to Spend Money

- Advertisers and influencers are purposefully trying to get you to spend more money than you have planned.

- For example, they may give you a sense of false urgency or make it easy to spend money.

Notice When and Where You Are Tempted

- Start paying attention to when and where you feel like making an impulse purchase. You might even try jotting down notes about when you feel tempted for a week – you could use paper or the notes app on a mobile device. See if you can identify any patterns.
- Set yourself up for success by controlling your environment. It helps to avoid temptation altogether when possible.
- Consider unfollowing or blocking people you follow on social media who tempt you to spend money or derail your effort on your goals.
- Unsubscribe from mailing lists that create urgency by sending you lots of deals or coupons.
- Check customer reviews.
- Use a list when you go shopping and stick to the list. Find a mantra that may help you stay focused, such as:

  If it is not on the list, it does not exist!

Build in a Pause

- You may be tempted to spend money on something you do not really need right now. Force yourself to pause so you can be sure it is not just an impulse.
- If you add an item to an online cart, shut down the browser before you purchase it. You can always come back later to buy it.
- If you are tempted to buy something you do not really need in a store, build in a pause. Do not put the item in your cart. You can come back at the end of your shopping trip to get it.
- Do not save your payment information at online retailers. Sometimes having to go find and input your payment information gives you enough time to resist the impulse.

Talk Yourself Out of It

When you are tempted to make a purchase that is not in your spending and saving plan, try asking yourself:

- Is this a want or a need?
- Does it help you reach your goals?
- Is this in your spending and saving plan?
- If it is not in your spending and saving plan now, can you plan for this expense by creating a savings goal?

- If you spend this money now, will it affect your ability to achieve your goals?
- Is there a way you would rather spend this money?

Talk yourself out of making an impulse purchase by reminding yourself of your goals.

Think about How Much Something Is Worth in Terms of Your Income

- Let us say your take-home pay is $100 each day. A $600 item would be worth 6 days of work.
- If you think of a new phone as costing "six full days of work," it might help you decide to postpone buying it now and set a financial goal to save money to buy it later.

Turning Goals into Financial Targets

For goals that require money to reach, you will want to know: How much do you need to set aside every week (or month) to meet your goal?

When figuring out how much you need to set aside every week to meet your goal, you need two pieces of information: the total amount you need to reach your goal and the number of weeks you have to reach your goal. Then, you can plug those two pieces of information into this formula:

Total amount needed for goal ÷ number of weeks = Amount to set aside each week for goal

(Source: "A Financial Empowerment Toolkit for Community Volunteers," Consumer Financial Protection Bureau (CFPB).)

CHAPTER 4

CAREER EXPLORATION AND SKILL DEVELOPMENT

About This Chapter: This chapter includes text excerpted from "Career Exploration & Skill Development," Youth.gov, October 15, 2016.

Finding a job can be a challenge for youth. They must determine what careers are available, what their interests are, and what skills they have or need to develop. Numerous resources are available to help youth get a sense of their interest and skills as well as gain employment experience and learn about employment opportunities.

Train for a Career

Career preparation should start in high school, but it should not end with graduation: Most occupations require some type of training or education after high school. On-the-job training, apprenticeships, certificates, nondegree awards, and various levels of college degrees are typically required for entry-level jobs.

Which type of training you need depends on the career you want to pursue. Your high school may offer opportunities for getting career training or college credits before you graduate. And after graduation, your training options expand even more. The closer you get to entering the workforce, the more you will want to narrow your choices.

(Source: "Career Planning for High Schoolers," U.S. Bureau of Labor Statistics (BLS), U.S. Department of Labor (DOL).)

Mentoring

Mentoring – matching youth or "mentees" with responsible, caring "mentors," usually adults – has been found to be an important support for youth as they transition to adulthood and the workforce. Mentoring provides opportunities for youth to develop emotional bonds with mentors who have more life experience and can provide support, guidance, and opportunities to help them succeed in life and meet their goals.

Mentoring relationships can be formal or informal, with substantial variation, but the essential components include creating caring, empathetic, consistent, and long-lasting relationships, often with some combination of role modeling, teaching, and advising. One form of mentoring, called "instrumental" or "topic-focused" mentoring, focuses on a particular problem and aims at helping mentees reach specific goals, such as improving academic performance or preparing for employment opportunities.

Career-focused mentoring, a type of instrumental or topic-focused mentoring, can take a variety of forms and may focus on different pieces of career development and employment. Some examples include assisting with the following:

- Writing resumes and cover letters
- Conducting mock interviews and providing support for answering interview questions
- Exploring possible careers and assisting with job, internship, or program searches
- Developing on-the-job skills (soft skills or technical skills)
- Modeling behavior, attitudes, or skills in the workplace (job-shadowing)
- Career planning and goal setting

Apprenticeships and internships can provide on-the-job opportunities to integrate mentoring into employment experiences for youth.

Assessment, Testing, and Counseling

Self-assessments help teach youth about themselves so that they can find a career that is a good fit for their interests and skills. They allow youth to explore:

- What they do and do not like
- How they react to certain situations
- Their skills
- Values

A professional, such as a counselor at a high school, trade or vocational school, college, or career training center, can help in selecting an appropriate assessment, interpreting the results, and providing career counseling.

The U.S. Department of Labor (DOL), Employment and Training Administration (ETA) sponsors two valuable resources to assist youth identify career pathways. CareerOneStop (www.careeronestop.org) is a website that provides a range of career-exploration help:

- Up-to-date information on job, salary and benefit information and related education and training opportunities
- Job search tools, resumes, and interview resources, and people and places to help jobseekers virtually, such as *What's My Next Move*, a guide to exploring careers for youth

The American Job Centers (AJCs), also known as "One Stop Centers," provide job referrals, counseling, and other supportive services to help with both job search and location of training and education resources. AJCs have locations across the United States.

The National Collaborative on Workforce and Disability (NCWD) provides a range of assessments that can help with the transition from school to employment. In addition to their focus on career planning, these resources recognize unique challenges faced by students with disabilities.

An additional online resource, Students and Career Advisors, allows students, career advisors, and parents to learn more about potential career opportunities. This resource provides opportunities for students to explore their interests, learn about potential careers, learn how to get job experience, and find additional educational opportunities to support career development.

Individualized Learning Plans

The goal of an Individualized Learning Plan (ILP), can also be known as "Individual Service Strategy" (ISS), is to connect what youth are doing in the classroom with their career and college goals and aspirations. ILPs help youth discover their skills and interests, match their interests with degrees and careers, set goals, and follow through in a thoughtful and meaningful way. The Office of Disability Employment Policy has a number of resources and information about ILP.

Job Search Assistance

Finding available jobs can be difficult. It is important for youth to recognize that finding a job often takes time and it is important to develop a plan, schedule, and goals when conducting a search. Many sources list available jobs, from newspapers to listservs to online directories. CareerOneStop (www.careeronestop.org) has online job listings that provide information on various employment options. Tools such as GetMyFuture (www.careeronestop.org/GetMyFuture), which allows youth to search for career opportunities based on past employment experiences, can help young people identify future careers that may be available based on their previous work experience. College career centers and CareerOneStop can help youth prepare their resumes, write cover letters, and practice interviewing. College career centers can also provide valuable resources for students as they search for jobs and internships.

Soft and Technical Skill Development and Training

Soft skills are generally defined as personal qualities, not technical, that translate to good job performance. They have been named by employers to be most important for successful job performance. Soft skills can be learned through a variety of means, including classroom instruction, youth programs, volunteering, and service learning.

More than 50 percent of manufacturers who completed the 2005 skills gap survey reported that technical skills will play an important role in meeting the needs of employers in the upcoming years. Vocational training courses or work-study programs can teach marketable technical or occupational skills. CareerOneStop can make referrals to local postsecondary institutions and youth-serving agencies when training and other services are needed. Not only are the people there know about these resources, but they also can approve vouchers to defray training costs. The Center for Employment Training (CET) is a nonprofit organization that has partnerships with the DOL. The CET has pioneered the practice of open-ended, competency-based training that uses the workplace as the context for simulations. The individualized training allows youth to train at their own pace and explore career options firsthand. The majority of training is provided through hands-on experience. The Office of Vocational and Adult Education within the U.S. Department of Education (ED) also helps states, schools, and community colleges support technical and vocational education.

Apprenticeships

Youth apprenticeship programs grew out of the school-to-work movement and offer youth classroom instruction combined with structured on-the-job training with a mentor. The training is split between academic courses and vocational training, while the on-the-job portion provides opportunities for practice in and understanding of work-based contexts for classroom instruction. Youth apprenticeships may lead to admission to adult registered apprenticeship programs after graduation. The DOL sponsors registered apprenticeship programs that meet its standards. The minimum requirement for participation in a registered apprenticeship program may vary by the skills demanded for the program, but to be eligible, youth must be at least 16. Because of restrictions, some hazardous jobs are limited to individuals over 18. Participation in apprenticeships allows youth to receive the following:

- **A paycheck.** From day one, youth earn a paycheck guaranteed to increase over time as they acquire new skills.
- **Hands-on career training.** Apprentices receive practical on-the-job learning in a wide selection of programs, such as healthcare, construction, information technology, and geospatial careers.
- **An education.** Apprentices receive hands-on learning and related instruction to supplement the hands-on-learning and have the potential to earn college credit, even an associate's or bachelor's degree, in many cases paid for by the employer.
- **A career.** Once the apprenticeship is completed, youth are on their way to successful long-term careers with competitive salaries and little or no educational debt.
- **National industry certification.** When an apprentice completes a Registered Apprenticeship program, she or he will be certified and can take that certification anywhere in the United States.
- **The opportunity to work with recognizable partners.** Many of the nation's most recognizable companies, such as CVS Health and UPS, have Registered Apprenticeship programs.

For an example of a youth apprenticeship program, visit the Wisconsin Department of Workforce Development (DWD): Youth Apprenticeship Program Information.

The Office of Disability Employment Policy (ODEP) provides a toolkit and other resources to increase the capacity of programs to provide integrated inclusive apprenticeship training to youth and young adults with a full range of disabilities, including those with the most significant disabilities. ODEP also provides guidance on how to use the increased flexibilities in the DOL apprenticeship regulations.

Internships

Internships, both paid and unpaid, provide youth with short-term, practical experiences to learn about careers, develop networks, and experience the workplace. The Wage and Hour Division at the DOL has identified six criteria to help determine whether interns must be paid the minimum wage and overtime under the Fair Labor Standards Act. Internships are available in a diverse array of career fields and can be formal or informal. Internships give youth the opportunity to explore what they like and do not like about certain careers. They allow youth who might not know what career they want to pursue with a chance to see whether a certain environment, job, or management style fits their needs. Both on-the-job experience and the application process allow youth to develop skills so that they are able to enter the job market with relevant career experience.

CHAPTER 5
WORKING DURING COLLEGE

About This Chapter: "Working during College," © 2017 Omnigraphics.

Working while in college may seem challenging, but it has its own perks. It can not only help students take care of their personal expenses but also provide opportunity to gain work experience. Some students have on-campus, work-study jobs that are part of a financial aid package. Others work at part-time, off-campus jobs to earn extra spending money. Many companies offer tuition assistance to help cover the cost of higher education for employees who want to increase their skills.

The biggest drawback to working during college is that jobs take time that you might otherwise spend studying, participating in extracurricular or social activities, or even sleeping. After all, working at a job for 10–20 hours per week is the equivalent of taking one to two additional classes. If the time commitment prevents you from taking a full load of classes, staying healthy, enjoying your college experience, or graduating on time, then working during college may not be worth it. However, employment during college also offers benefits that may outweigh the costs. Some of the advantages you may gain by working include the following:

- **Better academic performance.** Studies have shown that college students who work between 1 and 12 hours per week have higher graduation rates than students who do not work. The working students tend to perform as well or even better academically than their nonworking peers. Many students find that the business challenges and workplace issues they face in their jobs apply directly to their college classes and enhance the learning experience. Some students also use ideas from their college classes to solve problems in the workplace.
- **Time management skills.** Keeping up with the demands of college and a job forces you to manage your time effectively. You learn to stay organized, stick to a schedule, prioritize tasks, and develop good work and study habits. Building these critical time-management skills in college helps prepare you for a fast-paced, demanding career after graduation.

- **Less student-loan debt.** Most students who work during college do so in order to help pay for their education. Although many still need student loans to cover the costs of tuition and room and board, employment income can reduce the amount they need to borrow. By paying for books and basic living expenses out of their earnings, working students may be able to graduate with less student-loan debt than nonworking students.
- **More independence.** Some students must work to help cover education-related expenses. Others choose to work because they want to have cash available to spend on clothes, travel, eating out, entertainment, and other treats. If your parents are already paying for your education, you may feel guilty asking them for more funds. Earning your own spending money can give you greater independence. In addition, you can avoid the financial trap of applying for student credit cards to cover your extra expenses.
- **Money management skills.** Students who work during college gain valuable knowledge of personal finance. Earning an income allows you to take responsibility for establishing a budget, keeping track of expenses, paying bills, and managing your money. These skills will prove valuable once you graduate from college and launch your career.
- **Career experience.** Part-time jobs – even ones that may seem menial or meaningless – offer valuable work experience that can help you gain skills, build self-confidence, and meet potential references or networking contacts. Students who find part-time jobs or internships within their field of study also have an opportunity to clarify their career goals and add to the list of qualifications on their resumes. During job interviews, you can provide real-world examples of your ability to solve problems, work independently, and take responsibility. For many employers, work experience during college sets you apart from other recent graduates and improves your chances of landing a full-time job after graduation.

Starting with Smart Choices

Heading off to college is a time for new experiences, exploring academic interests, meeting new people and embracing newfound financial independence. However, financial independence comes with its share of risks and rewards. Are you prepared to make wise and informed financial decisions? Do you know how to recognize predatory credit offers? Can you properly manage a checking account? Do you have a savings plan? Do you understand your financial aid and how it will be repaid?

Smart financial choices you make today could help you achieve your future financial goals, like traveling or buying a car or home. However, money mistakes when you are just starting out can leave you in debt and negatively impact your credit score for a long period of time.

(Source: "Going to College," MyCreditUnion.gov.)

References

1. Dumbauld, Beth. "Six Things You Should Know about Working While Going to College," Straighter Line, October 20, 2016.
2. Higuera, Valencia. "Five Benefits of Working a Job While in College," Money Crashers, 2017.
3. Levy, David. "The Benefits of Working While in College," Edvisors, 2017.
4. Pros and Cons of Work-Study in College," The Prospect, 2014.

CHAPTER 6

SUMMER EMPLOYMENT: A SNAPSHOT OF TEEN WORKERS

Summer jobs offer teens the opportunity to explore the work environment. Although teens may work all year in different part-time jobs, the summer months provide an opportunity for teens to work on a full-time basis while schools are out of session. Hence, summer is the right time for teens to earn more money, get introduced to the 40-hour work week, and gain valuable experience, responsibility, and skills through summer employment.

Finding a Summer Job

Teens can identify job leads for summer employment through various sources:

- Internet
- Classified ads section in the local newspaper
- Job boards
- School counselors
- Recommendations from friends and family members

If you are interested in working at a specific place, then do not hesitate to contact the manager and inquire about possible job openings. Although there will likely be plenty of job openings for teens during the summer months, the competition will also be very high, so try to be the early bird. It is better to begin your job search well before the onset of summer.

Common Summer Jobs for Teens

There will be many openings in minimum-wage service industries for teenagers during the summer months. Before you jump into the process of job hunting, make a list of your likes and dislikes and try to find a job that suits you the best. Choosing the right summer job often sets you on the right career path in adulthood. Some common summer employment opportunities available for teens are as follows:

- **Camp counseling.** A camp counselor guides and mentors kids during outdoor camp programs and events. This job will suit older teens who are natural leaders and those who wish to spend more time outdoors.
- **Tutoring.** Some students use the summer months to catch up on school work and prepare for tests. Academically inclined teens can use this opportunity to teach such kids.
- **Golf caddying.** The game of golf picks up in the summer and there will be plenty of openings for golf caddying. This job involves a lot of walking and carrying heavy bags of golf clubs.
- Swimming pools/amusement parks are in action during the summer months. They provide job opportunities for teens in many areas, including ticket sales, park tours, swimming pool cleaning, food stalls, and so on. Teens who are strong swimmers can also work as lifeguards. Since lifeguarding is a challenging position with a lot of responsibility, it requires Red Cross certification.
- **Childcare.** Working parents often look for safe, secure, and reliable childcare for their young children during the months when school is not in session. Teens who enjoy spending time with children can consider babysitting or working at daycare centers.
- **Gardening.** Some people may not have the time or may be physically incapable of taking care of their lawns. Teens can assist them with planting, fertilizing, lawn mowing, and repairing irrigation systems. Gardening is in high demand during the summer months and may extend into the fall.
- **Retail sales.** Teens can find a great deal of opportunity as retail salespeople in fast-food restaurants, malls, grocery stores, and so on.
- **House sitting.** Many people travel during the summer vacation months and will be looking for responsible house sitters to look after their homes in their absence. The responsibilities of a house sitter include keeping the house clean, collecting mail and newspapers, watering plants, and taking care of the safety of the house.

Financial Empowerment

Financial empowerment is building the knowledge and ability of individuals to manage money and use financial services products that work for them.

Financially-empowered individuals are both informed and skilled. They know where to get help with their financial challenges and can access and choose financial products and services that meet their needs. This sense of empowerment can build confidence that they can effectively use their financial knowledge, skills, and resources to reach their goals.

(Source: "A Financial Empowerment Toolkit for Community Volunteers," Consumer Financial Protection Bureau (CFPB).)

Do Not Give Up

Some teens tend to give up too easily when they do not receive a reply from a potential employer after applying for a job. Persistent and polite follow ups can be an effective tool in such situations. However, due to heavy competition, not all teens end up getting a job. If you do not find a suitable job, you have other options to consider.

- **Volunteering** means providing service without getting paid. Teens can volunteer at schools, hospitals, and welfare organizations. Like paid jobs, you can find volunteering opportunities online.
- **Internships** are short-term, hands-on training opportunities offered by companies and businesses to bright students. Some internships may pay their interns a nominal salary, but most of them do not. However, if you perform well during the internship, then there is a good chance that you may be offered a full-time job.

Although most of the volunteering jobs and internships do not pay you a salary, they serve as a great way to build your knowledge and experience and look good on a resume. They can be helpful to land a high-paying job in the future.

References

1. "Teen Summer Jobs," *Houston Chronicle*, August 7, 2018.
2. "Finding a Summer Job or Internship," The Nemours Foundation/KidsHealth®, June 2017.
3. "15 Great Summer Jobs for Teens," Investopedia, May 12, 2017.
4. "Mistakes Teens Make in Looking for Summer or Part-Time Jobs," LiveCareer, January 4, 2013.

CHAPTER 7

UNDERSTANDING PAYCHECK AND PAY STATEMENT

About This Chapter: Text beginning with the heading "What Is a Paycheck?" is excerpted from "Your Paycheck," Federal Trade Commission (FTC), September 3, 2016; Text under the heading "What Is Included in a Typical Pay Statement?" is excerpted from "Your Income and Expenses," Federal Deposit Insurance Corporation (FDIC), April 9, 2021.

What Is a Paycheck?

Your paycheck is the money your employer pays you for doing your job. To get the money, you cash your paycheck at a business.

You can deposit your paycheck in your bank or credit union account. Or you can cash your paycheck with a bank, credit union, or another business.

What Is Direct Deposit?

Direct deposit is when your employer puts your paycheck into your bank or credit union account. Many employers offer direct deposit.

Tax

At the end of your first week on the job, you get your paycheck only to find out that a chunk of money is gone. Your employer has taken out – or withheld – the taxes you owe. Employers withhold money for federal income taxes, Social Security taxes, and state and local income taxes in some states and localities.

Taxes are payments of money to the government that provide public goods and services for the community. Some examples of public goods are national defense, street lights, and roads and highways. Public services include welfare programs, sanitation, law enforcement, and education.

(Source: "Your First Job," Internal Revenue Service (IRS).)

What Is a Pay Stub?

When you get a paycheck, you also get a pay stub. A pay stub is sometimes called an "earnings statement."

Your pay stub tells you:

- How much money you earned
- The time, or pay period, you are getting paid for
- What taxes and other money have been taken out, or deducted, from your pay

What Is Gross Pay?

Gross pay is all the money you earned at your job. But, you do not keep all of your gross pay. Your employer will take money out of your gross pay for taxes and benefits.

What Is Take-Home Pay?

Take-home pay, also called "net pay," is the money you get in your paycheck. Your employer takes money from your gross pay for taxes and benefits. The money left in your paycheck is your take-home pay.

What Is the Federal Insurance Contributions Act?

FICA stands for Federal Insurance Contributions Act. FICA is money the federal government takes out of your paycheck. This money is used for the government's Social Security and Medicare programs.

What Are Tax Withholdings?

The law says your employer must take money out of your paycheck for taxes. You can choose how much money to withhold from – or take out of – your paycheck. When you have a big change in your life, you might owe more or less money in taxes than before. To have the right amount of money come out of your paycheck for taxes, you change your withholdings.

What Is a W-2?

A W-2 is a form your employer sends you at the end of every year. A W-2 says how much money you earned during the year. Your W-2 also says how much money was taken out of your paycheck for taxes during the year. You use your W-2 when you file your taxes with the Internal Revenue Service (IRS) and some states.

How Often Will You Get a Paycheck?

Most jobs pay you either:

- Once a week
- Once every two weeks
- Once or twice a month

Where Can You Cash Your Paycheck?

Many businesses let you cash checks. Sometimes, they charge a fee. You can cash your paycheck at:

- Banks and credit unions
- Some convenience stores, grocery stores, and other stores
- Check-cashing stores

Cashing a paycheck at your bank or credit union is usually free. Sometimes, the bank named on the check might cash a paycheck if you do not have an account.

Businesses charge different fees for cashing a check. Call, visit, or go online to find out what a business charges.

Why Might You Use Direct Deposit?

If you use direct deposit, you get your money on pay day. You:

- Do not have to wait to cash or deposit your paycheck
- Get your cash without paying fees to cash your check
- Do not risk losing the check

To use direct deposit, you need to have a bank or credit union account. Ask your employer if it offers direct deposit. You might need to sign up for it.

Why Do You Bring Home Less Money Than You Earn?

Your employer takes out, or deducts, money for taxes before you get your paycheck. The law says that employers must deduct money for:

- State tax
- Federal tax
- FICA (Social Security and Medicare taxes)
- Disability or unemployment insurance

Employers also take out money for benefits, if you have them. They include:

- Health insurance
- A retirement savings account

Why Would You Want Your Employer to Take Out Money for Retirement Savings?

The money can grow in a retirement account until you retire. A 401(k) is one type of retirement account.

Some employers offer a match. A match means the employer will put extra money into your retirement account if you put some of your money into the account.

When Do You Need to Change Your Tax Withholdings?

Check your withholdings when you have a big change in your life. You might owe more or less money in taxes than before. You would want to withhold more money if you owe more in taxes. You would want to withhold less money if you owe less in taxes.

Changes that affect your taxes could be if you:

- Get married or divorced
- Have a baby
- Change your job

Talk to your employer or the human resources department if you have a big change.

What to Do?

Your paycheck is the money your employer pays you to do your job. You also get a pay stub, sometimes called an "earnings statement." A pay stub tells you how much you earned and how much money your employer took out for taxes and benefits.

How Do You Compare Fees to Cash Your Paycheck?

You can cash your paycheck at a business to get money in your hands. You might cash your paycheck at:

- A bank or credit union
- Some convenience stores, grocery stores, or other stores
- Check-cashing stores

Cashing a paycheck at your bank or credit union is usually free. Sometimes, the bank named on the check might cash a paycheck if you do not have an account.

Businesses charge different fees for cashing a check. Call, visit, or go online to find out what a business charges. Check-cashing stores sometimes charge high fees.

How Do You Sign Up for Direct Deposit?

Many employers will put your paycheck into your bank or credit union account. This is called "direct deposit." You do not have to pay fees to cash your check. You will get your money sooner.

Ask your employer if it has direct deposit. To sign up for direct deposit, give your employer information about your bank or credit union account.

What Do You Do with Your Pay Stubs?

Keep your pay stubs for a year. Your employer will send you a W-2 form each year. A W-2 form says how much money you earned during the year. Your W-2 also says how much money your employer took out for taxes. When you see that your W-2 is right, you can get rid of your pay stubs for that year.

Shred your pay stubs before you throw them away. Your pay stubs might have your Social Security number on them. Someone could use that to steal your identity.

What Is Included in a Typical Pay Statement?

Typical pay statements likely include these categories of information:

- **Personal information.** Information about you, such as your name and address.
- **Pay period.** The time period you are being paid for. It could be a week, two weeks, a month, or another time period. For example, the pay period could be December 1 to December 14.
- **Pay date.** The official date you receive the net pay. If you have direct deposit, you may get your net pay before the official pay date. There is often a delay between the end of the pay period and the pay date. Your pay date could be every Friday, or the 1st and 15th of every month, or perhaps every other Tuesday.
- **Gross pay.** How much money you earned during the pay period. The pay statement may also show year-to-date gross pay from this employer.
- **Deductions.** The amounts taken out of your gross pay. There are required deductions, such as Social Security, Medicare, and income taxes (federal and possibly state and local). There are also elective deductions, such as health insurance or union dues. Retirement account contributions could be required deductions or elective deductions. The pay statement may also show year-to-date deductions.
- **Net pay.** The amount of money you receive after all deductions are taken out of your gross pay. This is your take-home pay.
- **Employer contributions.** The amount the employer paid for benefits, such as health insurance. The pay statement may also show year-to-date employer contributions.
- **Balances for your personal time off, vacation, and sick leave.** These may also be included on the pay statement.

CHAPTER 8
BEING YOUR OWN BOSS

About This Chapter: Text beginning with the heading "Is Self-Employment for You?" is excerpted from "Self-Employment: What to Know to Be Your Own Boss," U.S. Bureau of Labor Statistics (BLS), U.S. Department of Labor (DOL), June 25, 2014; Text under the heading "Characteristics of Entrepreneurship" is excerpted from "Characteristics of Entrepreneurship," Small Business Administration (SBA), August 21, 2014.

Is Self-Employment for You?

People choose to become self-employed for many reasons, including greater independence and flexibility. But, they also consider the downsides, such as the long hours and lack of benefits.

As part of your decision-making process, you should weigh the pros and cons of starting a business, along with your own reasons for seeking self-employment. For example, hoping to make a lot of money quickly can lead you into trouble. But, if you feel passionately about developing an idea, self-employment may be right for you.

Rewards

For many self-employed workers, autonomy is the biggest reward. They are able to make their own decisions, such as what kind of work they do, whom they do it for, where and when they do it – and even how much to pay themselves.

Self-employed workers usually take on many different tasks, learning to do each as the need arises. For example, a self-employed barber needs to find a suitable location for opening a shop, attract clients, and price services, in addition to cutting hair.

Many workers find that self-employment allows them not only to expand their professional skills, but also to enrich themselves personally. "I learned a lot more about business and life than I ever expected," says Megan Lebon, a physician who owns a practice in Atlanta, Georgia.

Self-employment can bring other rewards, too. Some workers enjoy creating a new business and watching it grow. They feel good about working for something they believe in.

Challenges

Self-employment is hard work, especially during the first few years. Workers may have difficulty finding clients, earning a steady income, securing business loans, and navigating laws. These challenges add up to financial risk and uncertainty.

And, with income frequently unpredictable, workers may try to handle all or most parts of the business themselves. "You end up working a lot more than you think, oftentimes way more than when you were working for someone else," says Vicki James, owner of a marketing business in Rochester, New York. This schedule can make balancing work and personal life difficult.

Another challenge with self-employment is lack of benefits. Public and private employers typically contribute to retirement, health, and other benefits, offering affordable options to their employees. But, self-employed workers must find these benefits and pay for them entirely out of pocket. And there is no paid leave for vacation or illness: A day off work is a day without pay. These types of burdens may overstretch limited financial resources.

Get Started

Even after you choose an occupation for starting a business, becoming self-employed is not as easy as deciding to work for yourself. You need certain skills and a lot of preparation before you can focus on setting up and growing a business.

But, if getting started seems daunting, remember that you do not have to do everything at once and that help is available. Focus on taking one step at a time.

Skills and Knowledge

One of the most important requirements for self-employment, business experts say, is having the technical skills and knowledge you need to do the work you want to do. For example, a graphic design freelancer needs to know color theory and how to use design software. It is a bad idea to start a business in something you do not understand well.

Other technical skills, such as bookkeeping and marketing, are helpful for operating a business. You can learn these skills in a class, at school, with the help of a mentor, or on your own. Higher education, although not a prerequisite for success, is often useful.

Some occupations have specific entry requirements, regardless of whether workers are self-employed. Physicians, for example, must have a bachelor's degree and complete a medical degree program, residency, and licensure requirements. And real estate agents need to become licensed in their state.

Experts suggest that, in addition to having technical skills, you focus on improving "soft" skills, such as time management and people skills. And, regardless of what you do, having a passion for the work is key.

Time Management

Self-employed workers often have multiple responsibilities and keep long hours. Being able to manage time efficiently – for example, through multitasking and scheduling – is crucial. These skills help you determine how much time you need to complete tasks and whether you can take on additional work.

People Skills

Good people skills, such as communication and customer service, help you attract and retain both employees and clients – especially in the beginning. "Early on, you are the chief salesperson," says Dennis Wright, a small-business mentor in Santa Ana, California. "You have to sell people on your abilities and the value of your product or service."

Passion

Experts say that a passion for what you do can give you the belief, motivation, and commitment you need to overcome the challenges that self-employment may present. "You must like and be committed to what you are doing," Wright says, "or you are likely to give up when you hit bumps in the road."

Preparation

No matter how skilled and knowledgeable you are about the product or service you want to sell, you still need to prepare to ensure success in self-employment. Experts recommend that before you invest any money, you take some time to figure out what motivates you to become self-employed, do your research, and ask for help as you plan your business.

Understand Why

Experts say that self-employed workers often feel discouraged, especially when just getting started. Understanding your motivations for becoming self-employed can help sustain you in times of struggle. "The reasons why are the catalyst that will push you forward," says James. "They will help you overcome the moments of doubt."

The reasons for becoming self-employed differ for everyone. Consider what your reasons are, and make note of them. Then, refer to them when you face challenges, to remind yourself of why you pursued self-employment.

Research

Researching your potential business is a way of evaluating whether your idea is marketable. Through research, you can also learn more about your potential customers, competitors, and collaborators. Experts suggest examining the prospective market for your product or service so that you can answer essential questions, such as the following:

- Who and where is the customer?
- How can your potential customers benefit from the product or service you are offering?
- Who are your competitors?
- What will set you apart from your competition?

Professional journals, focus groups, surveys, business clubs, seminars, and current business owners are among the sources that can provide answers to these questions. You may even find reports written by people who have done similar research.

But, not every business idea is a winner. Experts suggest moving on when your research shows that an idea would not work. Your next idea might be the right one.

And be careful not to let research stop you from actually getting started. "I thought I first needed to know everything about running a business," James says. "Find the courage to make mistakes, and learn from them as you go."

Ask for Help

Many of the principles of business are the same, so people who have already had success with self-employment are often good sources of information to those who are considering it. They may share tips and mistakes, experts say, or make valuable suggestions you had not considered. "Learn from people smarter and more experienced than you," says Luyk.

Another possible advantage in asking for help is finding a mentor: someone who offers guidance, encouragement, advice, and emotional support throughout the life of your business. You may meet a potential mentor informally or through a business organization.

Setting Up Shop

After you have determined that your business idea is viable, it is finally time to set up shop, right? Not quite; you still have work to do. For starters, you need to write a business plan, ensure that you meet all legal and tax requirements, and prepare to limit your legal and financial liability. These steps also apply if you decide to freelance, even if you get started quickly out of your own home.

The process of setting up a business can be confusing and difficult. You will need to complete a lot of paperwork to ensure that you are complying with different laws and regulations, for example. Experts recommend consulting an accountant and a lawyer for help, and they say that this investment in your future business is money well spent. "Be upfront about what you want and what you can afford," says Luyk. "These professionals will save you money in the end."

Another difficulty is a lack of money early on. Experts suggest that, before you get started, you should save up enough money to last a couple of years so that you avoid financial pitfalls.

Write a Business Plan

A business plan describes what service you will provide or product you will make, along with how and when you will do it. "If you do not set goals, you would not achieve them," says business mentor Jack Bernard. "You will just chase your tail." Use your research to set goals for the business within specific timeframes. Your business plan should explain in detail every part of your business, including the following:

- Your business values and vision for the future
- Your business's strengths, weaknesses, opportunities, and threats
- Financial projections
- The experience and achievements of key staff

Business plans are important when you seek funding, which may include loans and grants. Most reputable creditors require applicants to have a business plan, a solid credit score, and a criminal background check before agreeing to lend or invest money in a business startup.

There are plenty of free resources available to help you write your plan. For example, you can find step-by-step guides and templates online or at your local library. And some business organizations offer individualized business counseling.

Meet Legal Requirements

To legally operate a business, you need a business license, as well as permits from the city and county, or both, in which the business is located. Local governments have many different requirements, but common ones include health and zoning permits.

You also need to meet Internal Revenue Service requirements. These include registering for an employer identification number, reporting wages and taxes withheld, and verifying employees' eligibility to work in the United States.

Other federal requirements may apply, depending on your business product or service. For example, a business that sells produce throughout the country needs a permit from the U.S. Department of Agriculture (USDA) to ensure that the food is safe.

Limit Liability

The way you structure your business affects your legal and financial responsibilities. For example, a sole proprietor is someone who owns a business and is accountable for all of its assets, obligations, and so on. And sole proprietors take a great risk by assuming all responsibility for their business; lenders can take control of personal assets of a sole proprietor who fails to repay a business loan.

Some business structures are designed to limit personal liability. The most common are a limited liability company (LLC) and an S corporation. Both of these arrangements protect personal assets by risking only what is invested in the business. Generally speaking, an LLC is easier to set up and manage, but an S corporation allows for the sale of business stock to investors.

Growing the Business

After you have completed the necessary steps for self-employment, you will need to focus on growing the business. Networking, staying competitive, making adjustments, and working through challenges will increase your chances of success.

Network

Experts say that networking is one of the best ways for self-employed people to spend their time. Among other benefits it provides, networking offers opportunities for self-employed workers to reach potential clients, meet business mentors, and test ideas to gauge interest. "You have to make yourself visible to your market," Lebon says. "People can only do business with you if they can find you first."

People usually network at business events, clubs, and meetings. Volunteering with a professional organization or serving on a community board also can be useful. And networking does not have to be formal. "Sometimes I just have coffee with people and share ideas, without worrying about business," says Ryan Schwartz, a freelance communications specialist in Portland, Oregon.

Some self-employed workers also use traditional marketing tools, such as creating a website or advertising in a local paper, to attract clients. But, experts caution against relying too heavily on marketing, which often is expensive and yields mixed results. "There is no better form of advertising than word of mouth," Wright says. "Give your customers a positive experience, and they will come back with a friend."

Stay Competitive

Competition is a part of being in business. To stay competitive with other businesses that are like yours, you have to stand out in areas such as price, quality, and service. "If you cannot define what makes you better," says Bernard, "your customers certainly would not know, and they will take their business elsewhere."

Updating your research will help keep you informed about competition in your market. After starting her cleaning business, for example, Luyk asked potential clients what they liked and disliked about their existing cleaning service. She used their feedback to improve her business.

When trying to set yourself apart from other small businesses, do not compete on price, say experts. Large businesses often offer lower prices because they have some advantages, such as the ability to buy in bulk at reduced cost, that small businesses do not. Lowering prices also reduces profit, which makes it harder to stay in business. "There's always someone willing to undercut your prices," says James. "Be better in other ways."

Make Adjustments

As your business evolves, it may outgrow your original vision. Keep up with developments by making adjustments, as necessary. For example, you may have planned to run your business from home for several years, but brisk sales might allow you to rent office space sooner than expected.

Experts often recommend adding workers to your payroll as one of the first tweaks you make after your business is established. "Hire people to help you as soon as you can afford them," says Luyk. "Then you can spend your time working on your business – not in the business."

It is important to hire employees who have experience and skills that you do not have. For example, opening an eatery to showcase your culinary skills can be risky if you have never run a restaurant. Employing a manager will offset your lack of management experience and let you focus on your strengths, such as cooking or designing the menu.

Persevere

Working for yourself is not easy. The business might take longer than you expect to turn a profit, for example, or you might have trouble making rent or paying your employees.

As most self-employed workers will tell you, it takes lots of preparation, determination, and time to achieve success in a new business. "This is a marathon," Lebon says. "Temper your expectations, take things one step a time, and do not give up."

Remember, experts say, you do not have a chance for success unless you take the first step. "People are so afraid to fail that they become paralyzed," says Luyk. "But you can learn a lot from failure. And if you do not try, you will always wonder what could have been."

Understanding Crowdfunding

Crowdfunding is a way to raise funds online by convincing a large number of people to each give money for a specific project or cause. This type of fundraising has become very popular, largely because it is easy to set up a crowdfunding campaign and raise money very quickly. And because of this, it is no surprise that crowdfunding sites have attracted scams.

Crowdfunding is often used by inventors to fund projects. In some cases, the inventor asks for small contributions – $10, $50, $100 – which can quickly add up to thousands of dollars in funding.

In other instances, the project creator hopes to get individual investors to give large amounts of money, perhaps in exchange for a reward once the project is completed. This can give small companies and entrepreneurs a chance to get their projects off the ground, letting them reach contributors directly.

(Source: "Understanding Crowdfunding," Federal Trade Commission (FTC).)

Characteristics of Entrepreneurship

Becoming a successful entrepreneur requires sound planning, creativity and hard work, and it also involves taking risks, because all businesses require some form of investment, usually time or money.

To begin evaluating whether launching your own business is right for you, consider some of the following common characteristics that are typical of successful small business owners:

Innovation and Creativity

The first step to starting a business is to come up with an idea or concept. It takes innovation to develop a product or service that brings value to customers that they cannot get elsewhere. Additionally, entrepreneurs often have to find creative ways to tackle everyday business problems like suppliers shipping inventory late and ineffective marketing plans.

Persistence and Resiliency

Businesses, like all things, take time to grow. Very few people will produce mass amounts of profit within just weeks or even months of being in business. There will be things that you fail at, even if your business is successful. Inevitably, some projects fail for a variety of reasons – poor planning, competitors offering better options, market timing or other factors. To be a successful entrepreneur you need to learn and grow from your mistakes to move forward. You must be able to live with uncertainty and overcome obstacles that you did not anticipate.

Flexibility

Even the most well thought out business plans will change along the way. Changes in the market, technology, and customer tastes are going to happen and they are out of your control. Your ability to be flexible and respond to these changes will be the key to your business's survival.

Passion

As you have probably realized, entrepreneurship is not easy. If you are not passionate about what you are doing, it will be much harder to persist through all of the challenges that come your way. Your customers will also notice, it is harder to sell something you are not passionate about yourself. Mollie Breault-Binaghi, who was named Vermont's Young Entrepreneur of the Year in 2011 by the SBA, said it best: "You have to be passionate about it. Otherwise it is not worth doing. Owning your own business is not easy and it is not going to make you rich quick. You are going to be in it for the long haul so it is got to be something you love."

Other characteristics that are helpful to an entrepreneur are persuasiveness, self-confidence, and being visionary. While it is not essential you have all of these qualities, it is a good idea to think about them and determine if entrepreneurship is really right for you.

CHAPTER 9
PREPARING A BUDGET

About This Chapter: Text in this chapter begins with excerpts from "Budgeting," Federal Student Aid (FSA), U.S. Department of Education (ED), August 5, 2015; Text beginning with the heading "Never Tried to Live on a Budget Before?" is excerpted from "Have You Not Tried to Live on a Budget Before?" Federal Student Aid (FSA), U.S. Department of Education (ED), April 10, 2014.

While you are in college or career school, you will need to learn how to manage your finances, plan for changes, and prepare for the unexpected. Budgeting will help you build decision-making skills and reach your financial and academic goals.

Why Should You Create a Budget?

A budget is a guide that keeps you on the path to reach your financial goals. Budgeting keeps your finances under control, shows when you need to make adjustments to your spending, and helps you decide where your money goes instead of wondering where it all went.

Budgeting helps you answer these important questions:

- Where does all my money go?
- Is there a way to spend less?
- How will I handle unexpected expenses such as replacing a broken cell phone or repairing my car?
- How can putting money into savings help me with some of my bigger financial goals?

Budgeting Helps You Achieve Academic and Financial Goals

Writing down your goals is the first step in creating a plan to make them realities. A budget will also help you prepare for unexpected expenses and obstacles. Budgeting involves challenging decision-making, but setting goals will make the tough choices a little easier.

As you create a budget, you will want to set short-, medium-, and long-term goals and track your progress toward achieving them.

Short-Term Goals

Budgeting helps you achieve academic and financial goals.

Medium-Term Goals

Medium-term goals involve thinking a bit farther into the future, perhaps the next one to three years. These goals could include buying a new laptop computer, saving $1,000 for an emergency fund, completing your program of study, or saving $5,000 for a down payment on a car.

Long-Term Goals

What do you want to do beyond three years and into the future? Long-term goals could include paying off your student loans after graduation, saving toward a down payment on a house, or saving for retirement.

Budgeting Makes It Easier to Plan, to Save, and to Control Your Expenses

When you set up your budget, you will be able to see whether your expenses exceed your income and, if so, then you can identify expenses that can be reduced. Once you are paying attention to your income and spending, you can make informed decisions that will help you meet your financial goals.

Plus, if you have problems keeping your spending under control, a budget will help you manage your spending. Following a budget can help you free up money for the things that really matter to you.

Budgeting Can Help You Avoid Debt and Improve Your Credit

When you stick to a budget, you avoid spending more than you earn and you can avoid or reduce your credit card debt. If you have received student loans to help with the cost of college or career school, then a budget will help you make the most of the money you have borrowed and can help you determine how long it will take to repay your debt and how much it will cost. If you do borrow, being able to pay what you owe on time each month will have a positive impact on your creditworthiness and your financial future.

How Do You Create a Budget?

Creating a budget is pretty straightforward and starts with this simple equation:

What you earn (your income) minus what you spend (your expenses).

The steps involved in creating a budget include:

- Determining your timeframe and setting goals,
- Finding a budgeting tool that works for you,
- Identifying your income and expenses,
- Subtracting your expenses from your income to see if you have money left over or if you have a shortfall, and
- Making any needed adjustments.

Budgeting is not just a one-time event. You will need to track your spending over time and update your budget as needed.

How Do You Balance a Job and School?

For some students, working while in college is a necessity; for others, it is a way to build a résumé or earn extra money for luxuries. Whatever the reason, it is important to know the pros and cons of working while you are attending school.

If you have a job, determine how many hours a week you will be able to work and still be able to stay on track with school demands. For example, if you want to earn more money and potentially reduce your need for student loans (or reduce the amount that you borrow), then you could consider working more hours. Managing a schedule with limited free time is an excellent way to prepare for your future. But remember, you may also need to take fewer classes to accommodate your work schedule. Keep in mind that part-time enrollment will delay your graduation, postpone your ability to earn a higher income, and possibly impact your eligibility for some federal aid. Tuition and fees may also be higher for part-time enrollment.

You may opt to work fewer hours and maximize the benefit of your student loans by taking a heavier class load instead of the minimum requirements. By taking extra classes, you may be able to graduate earlier. Alternatively, you may find that taking classes during the summer leaves you better able to balance work and school during the academic year and still stay on track to graduate on time. Keep in mind that the longer it takes to complete your program of study, the more you will pay in total.

What Should You Know about Budgeting after You Leave School?

Your expenses will change after you leave school. For example, if you recently graduated, you usually would not be required to begin paying off your student loans for six months, but when that payment is added to your monthly expenses, it will have a big impact on your budget. When you leave school, you will want to update your budget to include student loan payments, as well as your new income and living costs. Leaving school can be an exciting (and stressful) time, but you do not want to stop tracking and managing your finances.

As you move through changes in your life, you will need to constantly reevaluate your income and expenses. Your goals will change as well. You may want to buy a car, get married, have children, continue your education, or start a business, and all these activities affect your budget in some way. Think of your budget as a living document. You have the power to revise it at any time to keep track of your finances and reach your goals.

Have You Not Tried to Live on a Budget Before?

Get tips to help you start budgeting, manage your budget, and stay on track.

As you create and maintain your budget, you will want to keep some important tips and suggestions in mind.

Get Started

Here are some important points to keep in mind as you build your budget and identify what goes into your income and expenses.

- **Overestimate your expenses.** It is better to overestimate your expenses and then underspend and end up with a surplus.
- **Underestimate your income.** It is better to end up with an unexpected cash surplus rather than a budget shortfall.
- **Involve your family in the budget planning process.** Determine how much income will be available from family sources such as parents or your spouse. Discuss how financial decisions will be made.
- **Prepare for the unexpected by setting saving goals to build your emergency fund.** Budgeting will help you cover unusual expenses and plan for changes that may happen while you are in school.
  - Planning to move off campus? Short-term budgeting goals for the year can include saving for the rent deposit and furniture for your new apartment.
  - Starting an internship next semester? Adjust your budget to save for buying new clothes to wear to work and paying increased transportation costs.
  - Finishing school in the next year? Budget to include job search expenses such as résumé preparation, travel to interviews and job fairs, and professional exam fees. Also, you may need to think about how you will manage your money between leaving school and finding a job – this is a time when an emergency fund can really help out.

Differentiate between Needs and Wants

One benefit of budgeting is that it helps you determine if you have the resources to spend on items that you want versus those you need.

- Start by making a list of things you would like to save up for.
- Identify whether each item on the list is something you absolutely need or is really a want.
- If you decide you want something, ask yourself if you will still be happy you bought the item in a month.
- Next, prioritize each item on the list.
- Once you have set your priorities, you can then determine whether you should incorporate each item into your budget.

Table 9.1. Needs and Wants

First Step Your Needs and Wants	Second Step Need or Want?	Third Step Priority Importance? 1=must have 2=really want 3=would be nice
Save for a vacation	Want	3
Buy a new computer	Want	2
Go to college	Need	1
Buy a better car	Want	2
Save for an emergency fund	Need	1
Save money for a down payment on a house	Need	3
Pay off credit cards	Need	1

Pay Yourself First!
Include "Savings" as a recurring expense item in your monthly budget. Small amounts that you put away each month do add up.

Manage Your Budget

Keeping track of all of your spending may seem like a lot of work. But if you are organized, keep good records, and use some of the following tips, you will find it is easier than you may think. And, do not be too hard on yourself if you slip up.

- **Record your actual expenses.** Have you noticed how fast your cash disappears? To get a handle on where you cash is going, carry a small notebook or use a phone app to record even the smallest expenditures such as coffee, movie tickets, snacks, and parking. Some expenses that are often ignored include music downloads, charges for extra cell phone usage, and entertainment expenses. Search for an online tool to assist you – many are free!
- **Organize your records.** Decide what system you are going to use to track and organize your financial information. There are mobile apps and computer-based programs that work well, but you can also track your spending using a pencil and paper. Be sure to be consistent and organized, and designate a space to store all your financial information. Good record-keeping saves money and time!
- **Create a routine.** Manage your money on a regular basis, and record your expenses and income regularly. If you find that you cannot record your

expenses every day, then record them weekly. If you wait longer than two weeks to record information, you may forget some transactions and be overwhelmed by the amount of information you need to enter.

- **Include a category in your budget called "unusual."** There will be some expenses every month that would not fall neatly into one category or that you could not have planned for. An "Unusual" category will help you budget for these occasional expenses.
- **Review your spending for little items that add up to big monthly expenditures.** The daily cup of coffee and soda at a vending machine will add up. Consider packing your lunch rather than eating out every day. Spending $10 a day eating out during the week translates to $50 a week and $200 a month. A $5 packed lunch translates into a savings of $1,200 a year. Save even more by looking for ways to manage and reduce your transportation and entertainment expenses.
- **Make your financial aid credit balance refund last.** If your school applies your financial aid to your tuition and fees and there is money left over, the school will refund that money to you so you can use it for other education-related expenses (textbooks, transportation, food, etc.). Remember that your financial aid is supposed to help you cover your cost of attendance for the whole semester or term, so be sure to make that refund stretch over time rather than spending it all as soon as you get it.
- **Comparison shop.** Comparison shopping is simply using common sense to compare products in an attempt to get the best prices and best value. This means doing a little research before running out to buy something, especially when it comes to more expensive items. Make the most of tools like phone apps for comparing prices and value.
- **Use credit cards wisely.** Think very carefully before you decide to get your first credit card. Is a credit card really necessary, or would another payment option work just as well? If you receive a credit card offer in the mail, do not feel obligated to accept it. Limit the number of cards you get.
- **Do not spend more on your credit card than you can afford to pay in full on a monthly basis.** Responsible use of credit cards can be a shopping convenience and help you establish a solid credit rating and avoid financial problems. Consider signing up for electronic payment reminders, balance notices, and billing statement notifications from your credit card provider.

CHAPTER 10
PAYING BILLS

About This Chapter: This chapter includes text excerpted from "Ways to Pay Your Bills," Consumer Financial Protection Bureau (CFPB), July 31, 2015.

When you move to a new place, it does not take long for bills to start coming.

You may pay some bills such as rent, utilities, and other payments each month. You may also have one-time bills, such as a security deposit when you rent an apartment.

In many cases, you will have one or more options you can choose from to make these payments. The list below helps you understand different bill payment options and their potential advantages and disadvantages. Knowing how they work could help you avoid some fees, including fees from late or missed payments.

Tips

- Make a list of your bills and their due dates, and put them on a calendar so you can easily see when payments are due.
- Some creditors let you pick the day of the month that you bill is due.
- However you choose to pay your bills, keep track of your money coming in and going out. It will help you avoid fees.

Check

Checks are forms that you fill out to pay for something from a checking account.

You write the amount and the name of the person or company that you wish to pay on the check. The amount comes out of your bank checking account when the person or company who receives the check deposits it or cashes it. You can also get a similar account from a credit union.

Benefits

- Convenient once you apply for and the account is set up at a bank or credit union.

- Can be mailed.
- Easy to prove payment if there is a dispute.
- Funds are held in the checking account until you write out the check and the check is deposited.
    - Unlike cash, if a check is lost or stolen or someone forges your signature, you have protection for the money in your account. But, it can be hard to stop a check if the person who receives it deposits it quickly.

Risks

- If you pay bills by check without enough money in your account, the bank or company you send the check to may charge you fees.
- You have to remember to pay a bill using a check each time it is due (not automated).
- Postage costs of mailing the payment

Automatic or Direct Debit

You provide the merchant or service provider (e.g., your cell phone provider or utility company) with your checking account information and they take the funds from your account each time the bill is due (e.g., every month).

Benefits

- Convenient, saves time and free.
- You may pay a lower interest rate for loans if you make your payments via automatic debit.
- Makes it easy to pay for bills that are frequent and consistent.
- Reduces the chance of being late – once you set it up, it is automatic.
- You have the right to end automatic payments.
- Easier to prove payment should a dispute arise.
- If the amount of the bill changes each month you may get a notice before the transfer is made to pay the bill.

Risks

- If you pay bills by automatic debit without enough money in your account, the bank or company you are paying to may charge you fees.

Warning: When money is automatically taken from your account, you could accidentally spend more than you have. If you do not have enough money in your account to cover an automatic payment or other charges you have made, you may have to pay costly fees. To stop automatic withdrawals, contact both the merchant and your bank

Online Bill Payment

You give your bank the merchant or service provider's information, and your bank makes the payment according to the amount and schedule you set up.

Benefits

- Convenient and saves time.
- Makes it easy to pay for bills that are frequent and consistent.
- You can choose between making one-time payments each billing cycle or setting up recurring (automatic) payments using your bank or credit union's online web services.
- Reduces the chance of being late – once you set it up, it is automatic.
- Easier to prove payment should a dispute arise.
- Easier to stop an unintended or erroneous payment.

Risks

- Takes time to set up and learn.
- If you pay bills by online bill payment without enough money in your account, the bank or service provider may charge you fees.
- If you have set up recurring payments and the amount changes, you may pay the wrong amount. If you pay less than the full amount of the bill, you may have to pay fees.

Money Order

A money order can be used instead of a check. You can buy a money order to pay a business or other party.

Benefits

- Easy to understand.
- Can be mailed.
- No personal banking information appears on the money order.

Risks

- May be inconvenient because you have to buy a money order.
- Cost to buy money order and to mail the payment.
- May be hard to prove payment unless you have the money order receipt and a receipt for payment.
- Funds are difficult or impossible to recover if lost or stolen.
- You have to remember to pay the bill each time it is due (not automated).

Credit Card

A credit card allows you to borrow money up to an approved credit limit. You will pay interest if you carry a balance, and you can be charged other fees based on the terms of the contract. You can expect to make a minimum monthly payment and you may want to pay more than the minimum to pay it off sooner.

Benefits

- Can use a credit card to pay bills over the phone or online.
- Easy to prove payment should a dispute arise.
- Protects you from having to pay for some or all the charges if your card or information is stolen or lost and you report the theft.
- Can be set up to automatically pay recurring bills.
- Can help build your credit history if you make payments on time and do not get close to your credit limit.

Risks

- Costs more than paying for the purchase with cash or a check if you cannot pay the credit card balance in full every month. If you carry a balance, you have to pay interest on the balance.
- Creates another bill you have to pay.
- Creates debt – you are borrowing money to pay for bills and other items.

Cash

Cash is money that you have in hand.

Benefits

- Often no fees associated with paying cash directly to the company if paying the full amount owed. Buying or using a special product such as a money order or prepaid cards may cost money.
- When you use cash, you are not incurring debt.
- No risk of overdrawing your account.

Risks

- Not all bill payments can be made in cash.
- Can be inconvenient and costly to travel to the company to pay the bill in person.
- May be hard to prove payment unless you have a receipt.
- Cash is difficult or impossible to recover if lost, stolen or destroyed.
- You have to remember to pay the bill each time it is due (not automated).

CHAPTER 11

SAVING MONEY WHEN YOU SHOP

About This Chapter: This chapter includes text excerpted from "Saving Money When You Shop," Federal Trade Commission (FTC), September 28, 2012.

What Does It Mean to Save Money When You Shop?

Saving money means that you find ways to pay less money when you shop. Saving money means paying the best price for the things you want to buy.

Can You Save If You Always Buy the Cheapest Product

No. Saving money does not mean always buying the cheapest product. The quality of the product you are buying matters, too. Sometimes, something that costs a little more money will last longer. That might make it a better value.

For example:

- If you buy one pair of shoes. That pair of shoes will last one year. Or, you could buy a new pair of shoes every six months.
- The shoes that last a year cost $50. The shoes that last six months cost $30 a pair, which is $60 a year.
- In a year, you might save $10 by spending more on shoes that last longer.

What Are Coupons?

A coupon offers a deal on certain products or at certain stores. A coupon might be a piece of paper that you cut out of the newspaper or a magazine. A coupon also might be a code you enter on a website.

What Can You Do to Save Money When You Shop?

A good way to save money is to compare prices. You compare prices by looking at the price of something at more than one store. Something might be "on sale" at one store. But, another store might sell the same thing for less money.

Figure 11.1. Coupons
You pay $45.
You saved $10.

When you are shopping, you can ask:

- **What is the best price you can give me?** The store might give you a lower price.
- **Will this item go on sale soon?** You might be able to wait for the sale and save money.

Sometimes, you might find a better price online. When you see a price online, find out if you will need to pay extra money to have it sent to you. This cost is called "shipping." If you add the shipping cost to the price, is it still a good deal?

Do Coupons Really Help You Save Money?

A coupon can help you save money on certain products or at certain stores. But, coupons can help you save only if you are buying something you need. Do not buy things just because you have a coupon for them.

For example:

Here is an example of how a coupon works:

- The clothes you want cost $55 (plus tax)
- Your coupon is for $10 off a $50 purchase
- Your purchase is more than $50.

Where Do You Find Coupons?

You can cut coupons out of the newspaper or a magazine. You also can find coupons online at:

- The website for the company that makes the product
- Websites for stores that sell the product
- Coupon websites that list coupons for lots of stores

To use a coupon online, you often need to type your "coupon code" or "promotional code" into a box. This happens while you are "checking out" and entering the information to pay for what you are buying.

What Else Should You Know about Coupons?

Some stores have "double coupon" days. On these days, you might get twice as much money off.

For example, if you have a coupon for 50 cents off of a certain brand of orange juice, you would get $1 off on double coupon days.

Look for double coupon days at grocery stores. Ask at the store whether they have double coupon days.

Many coupons have an "expiration date." After that date, you cannot use the coupon.

Should You Always Wait for Things to Go on Sale?

A "sale" is when a store sells something for a cheaper price. Sometimes you can wait for an item to go on sale. That way, you do not have to pay as much for it.

Before you buy an item that is "on sale," ask yourself:

- Would you want to buy this if it were not on sale?
- Are there other products like this that you like better?
- Have you checked the price at other stores? Is the "sale" price the best one?
- Do you have the money to buy this, even at the lower sale price? Will buying this add to my debt?
- If you do not buy this, what could you use the money for instead?

A sale price is not a good price if you do not need the item. A sale price does not help you save money if you cannot afford to buy the item.

Impulse Buying

Impulse buying is when you decide to make a purchase on the spur-of-the-moment, without planning ahead or taking into consideration whether you really need or can afford the item. Everyone makes impulsive purchases once in a while. You might grab a pack of gum while waiting in the supermarket checkout line, for instance, or give in to the urge to buy a shirt that is on sale. Although this common behavior is not always dangerous or harmful, it can create problems if it becomes excessive or out of control.

There are many psychological factors that can feed your desire to buy things. Social and cultural factors can also influence your spending decisions. In addition, most retail stores and websites are specifically designed to encourage impulse buying. But, recognizing your personal triggers and warning signs can help you resist the urge and control your spending. Since impulse buying can lead to anxiety, buyer's remorse, unhappiness, and debt, avoiding it can improve your emotional well-being as well as your financial health.

(Source: "Impulse Buying," © 2017 Omnigraphics.)

What to Do?

You can save money when you shop if you compare prices at different stores, use coupons, think about whether you really want something, and ask questions.

How Do You Start Saving?

Before you buy something, ask yourself:

Have you:

- Looked for coupons?
- Checked the price at more than one store?
- Asked about when it might go on sale, or thought about waiting for a sale?
- Thought about what else you might spend your money on if you do not buy it?

When You Find a Good Deal, Should You Buy the Product?

Maybe you should buy it. Maybe not. Before you buy, think about whether this is the right deal for you.

Ask yourself:

- Are you buying this just because it is on sale?
- Do you really want or need this thing?
- Can you afford this product, even on sale?
- Do you want to buy it, even if it adds to your credit card debt?

PART 2 | SAVING AND INVESTING STRATEGIES

CHAPTER 12

ROADMAP TO SAVING AND INVESTING

About This Chapter: This chapter includes text excerpted from "Save and Invest," Inverstor.gov, U.S. Securities and Exchange Commission (SEC), April 4, 2011.

Define Your Goals

Knowing how to secure your financial well-being is one of the most important things you can do for yourself. You do not have to be a genius to do it. You just need to know a few basics, form a plan, and be ready to stick to it.

To end up where you want to be, you need a financial plan. Ask yourself what you want. List your most important goals first. Decide how many years you have to meet each specific goal, because when you save or invest, you will need to find an option that fits your time frame. Here are some tools to help you decide how much you will need to save for various needs.

Figure Out Your Finances

Take an honest look at your entire financial situation – what you own and what you owe. This is a "net worth statement." On one side, list what you own. These are your "assets." On the other side, list what you owe. These are your "liabilities" or "debts." Subtract your liabilities from your assets. If your assets are larger than your liabilities, you have a "positive" net worth. If your liabilities are larger than your assets, you have a "negative" net worth.

You will want to update your "net worth statement" every year to keep track of how you are doing. Do not be discouraged if you have a negative net worth – following a financial plan will help you turn it into positive net worth.

The next step is to keep track of your income and expenses. Write down what you and others in your family earn and spend each month, and include a category for savings and investing. If you are spending all your income, and never have money to save or invest, start by cutting back on expenses. When you watch where you spend your money, you will be surprised how small everyday expenses can add up. Many people get into the habit of saving and investing by paying themselves first. An easy way to do this is to have your bank automatically deposit money from your paycheck into a savings or investment account.

Small Savings Add Up to Big Money

How much does a daily candy bar cost? Would you believe $465.84? Or more?

If you buy a candy bar every day for $1, it adds up to $365 a year. If you saved that $365 and put it into an investment that earns 5 percent a year, it would grow to $465.84 by the end of five years, and by the end of 30 years, to $1,577.50. That is the power of "compounding."

With compound interest, you earn interest on the money you save and on the interest that money earns. Over time, even a small amount saved can add up to big money.

If you buy on impulse, make a rule that you will always wait 24 hours before buying anything. You may lose your desire to buy it after a day. Also, try emptying your pockets at the end of each day and putting spare change aside. You will be surprised how quickly those nickels and dimes add up.

Pay Off Credit Cards or Other High Interest Debt

No investment strategy pays off as well as, or with less risk than, eliminating high interest debt. Most credit cards charge high interest rates – as much as 18 percent or more – if you do not pay off your balance in full each month. If you owe money on your credit cards, the wisest thing you can do is pay off the balance in full as quickly as possible. Virtually no investment will give you returns to match an 18 percent interest rate on your credit card. That is why you are better off eliminating all credit card debt before investing. Once you have paid off your credit cards, you can budget your money and begin to save and invest.

Here are some tips for avoiding credit card debt:

Put Away the Plastic

- Do not use a credit card unless you know you will have the money to pay the bill when it arrives.

Know What You Owe

- It is easy to forget how much you have charged on your credit card. Every time you use a credit card, track how much you have spent and figure out how much you will have to pay that month. If you know you will not be able to pay your balance in full, try to figure out how much you can pay each month and how long it will take to pay the balance in full.

Emergency Fund

An emergency fund or a rainy day fund can be an important part of your savings plan. Having your own money set aside to cover unexpected expenses can save you money, because you will not pay interest, fees, or other costs that come from borrowing the money you need.

How much should you save? Start with $500 as your goal. This is enough to cover a lot of common emergencies: many car repairs, a plane ticket to care for a sick family member, or to pay minor medical costs. Once you reach $500, consider reaching for $1,000. This may be enough to cover your rent if you lose your job, take care of major car repairs, and pay for many household repairs.

(Source: "A Financial Empowerment Toolkit for Community Volunteers," Consumer Financial Protection Bureau (CFPB).)

Pay Off the Card with the Highest Rate

- If you have got unpaid balances on several credit cards, you should first pay down the card that charges the highest rate. Pay as much as you can toward that debt each month until your balance is once again zero, while still paying the minimum on your other cards. The same advice goes for any other high-interest debt (about 8 percent or above), which does not offer any tax advantages.

Save for a Rainy Day

Savings are usually put into safe places that allow you access to your money at any time. Examples include savings accounts, checking accounts, and certificates of deposit. Your money may be insured by the Federal Deposit Insurance Corporation (FDIC) or National Credit Union Administration (NCUA). But, there is a tradeoff between security and availability; your money earns a low interest rate.

Most smart investors put enough money in savings to cover an emergency, such as sudden unemployment. Some make sure they have up to six months of their income in savings so that they know it will absolutely be there for them when they need it.

But, how "safe" is a savings account if the interest it earns does not keep up with inflation? Let us say you save a dollar when it can buy a loaf of bread. But, years later when you withdraw that dollar plus the interest you earned, it might only be able to buy half a loaf. That is why many people put some of their money in savings, but look to investing so they can earn more over longer periods of time.

Understand What It Means to Invest

When investing, you have a greater chance of losing your money than when you save. Unlike FDIC-insured deposits, the money you invest in securities, mutual funds, and other similar investments are not federally insured. You could lose your "principal," which is the amount you have invested. That is true even if you purchase your investments through a bank. But when you invest, you also have the opportunity to earn more money. On the other hand, investing involves taking on some degree of risk.

Diversify Your Investments

Diversification can be neatly summed up as, "Don't put all your eggs in one basket." The idea is that if one investment loses money, the other investments will make up for those losses. Diversification cannot guarantee that your investments will not suffer if the market drops. But, it can improve the chances that you will not lose money, or that if you do, it will not be as much as if you were not diversified.

Gauge Your Risk Tolerance

What are the best saving and investment products for you? The answer depends on when you will need the money, your goals, and whether you will be able to sleep at night if you purchase a risky investment (one where you could lose your principal).

For instance, if you are saving for retirement, and you have 35 years before you retire, you may want to consider riskier investment products, knowing that if you stick to only the "savings" products or to less risky investment products, your money will grow too slowly. Or, given inflation and taxes, you may lose the purchasing power of your money. A frequent mistake people make is putting money they will not need for a very long time in investments that pay a low amount of interest.

On the other hand, if you are saving for a short-term goal, five years or less, you do not want to choose risky investments, because when it is time to sell, you may have to take a loss.

Learn about Investment Options

While the SEC cannot recommend any particular investment product, a vast array of investment products exists, including stocks, mutual funds, corporate and municipal bonds, annuities, exchange-traded funds (ETFs), money market funds, and U.S. Treasury securities.

Stocks, bonds, mutual funds and ETFs are the most common asset categories. These are among the asset categories you would likely choose from when investing in a retirement savings program or a college savings plan. Other asset categories include real estate, precious metals and other commodities, and private equity. Some investors may include these asset categories within a portfolio. Investments in these asset categories typically have category-specific risks.

Before you make any investment, understand the risks of the investment and make sure the risks are appropriate for you. You will also want to understand the fees associated with the buying, selling, and holding the investment.

CHAPTER 13

MANAGING DAILY EXPENSES AND SAVING FOR YOUR GOALS

About This Chapter: Text in this chapter begins with excerpts from "Budget Planning Strategies," AmeriCorps, May 10, 2021; Text under the heading "Managing Your Living Allowance: Everyday Savings" is excerpted from "Managing Your Living Allowance: Everyday Savings," AmeriCorps, March 28, 2021; Text under the heading "How Else Can You Save Money?" is excerpted from "Making a Budget," Federal Trade Commission (FTC), September 28, 2012.

Living on a fixed stipend that is near the poverty line can be stressful. Planning your budget ahead of time can help to reduce that stress, prepare you for your year of service, and anticipate areas of concern or change.

Creating a custom budget for yourself requires some time and planning. Think of your budget as your own, personal plan – one size does not fit all! Start out by considering your budget at a high level. By following these strategies, you will be better prepared to customize your budget in more detail.

Here are some things to think about when beginning to plan your budget:

Determine Your High-Level Goal(s)

High-level goals are "big picture" tasks you want to accomplish.

Examples:

- Spend less money than you earn.
- Pay down existing debt.
- Save money for a specific purchase or life transition.

Establish Specific Benchmarks

Benchmarks branch out from your high-level goals. Make them as specific as possible so you can measure your progress.

Example:

- Instead of "I will spend less going out this month," create specific benchmarks, such as, "I will only spend $25 on entertainment each week" or "I will deposit an extra $50 into my savings each month."

Make Sure Your Goals/Benchmarks Are Realistic

Example:

- If you pay $650 in rent and $100 in utilities, you might have a hard time keeping your monthly spending below $1,000. Make sure your goal is one that you can actually achieve, to avoid setting yourself up for failure or frustration.

Track Your Spending

Examples:

- Examine your pay stubs closely to determine your exact monthly income.
- Review your last three bank statements to determine how much you typically spend each month.
- Decide on a method or tool for tracking spending and monitor your progress toward your goal. Consider the classic "envelope method," in which you withdraw only the cash you need for the week, and place predetermined amounts for each spending category into an envelope. When the envelope is empty, you are done spending in that category.
- Sign up for a free budgeting app. Budgeting programs are available online and on mobile devices. You can sync them to your bank accounts and keep track of your spending in real time.

Set a Time Limit

Example:

- Consider a 21-day financial fast. Three weeks is a reasonable period of time to cut back on your wants and focus only on your needs. After 21 days you can create a long-term plan that you know you will be comfortable sticking with. Whether you fast or not, it is helpful to set a deadline for yourself to check in on how you are doing.

Managing Your Living Allowance: Everyday Savings

As you work on ways to manage your budget and your overall finances, do not forget to focus also on ways to cut costs and build your savings. It is something you can do every day. It all starts with a plan that includes deliberate goals for budget reductions and putting away that extra money. And as we all know, unexpected expenses and situations can occur that require us to spend money where we did not intend! Saving money and thinking proactively about where costs can be reduced can bring you greater peace of mind as you focus on your year of service.

Making Savings Automatic

If you receive a regular paycheck, one way to build savings is through direct deposit into a bank account or onto a payroll card or by setting up a system of savings.

- **Using direct deposit saves you both time and money.** You do not have to get your check cashed to use it. And the funds are generally available as soon as they are deposited. That means you get paid on time, even if you are not working on payday, and that you get paid at the start of the payday, not the end of the day.
- **If you have a bank account, you can arrange to have some of the deposited money moved automatically to a savings account.** If your weekly paycheck of $245 is directly deposited into your checking account every week, you can have $10 automatically transferred into a savings account. Once you set this system up, you may forget about that $10. And by the end of the year, you will have over $500 in that account.

(Source: "A Financial Empowerment Toolkit for Community Volunteers," Consumer Financial Protection Bureau (CFPB).)

Cutting Costs and Saving Money Can Help You

- Reduce worry and fear of being unprepared for expenses.
- Set savings goals that are realistic for your budget.
- Find ways to stop overpaying for common expenses such as utilities, food, and clothing.
- Discover great resources for helping you save every day.

How Else Can You Save Money?

You can try these ways to help save money:

- For one month, write down everything you spend. Small expenses, like a cup of coffee, can add up to a lot of money. When you know where you are spending your money, you can decide what you might not want to buy.
- Pay with your credit card only if you can pay the full amount when the bill comes. That way, you do not pay interest on what you owe.
- Pay your bills when they are due. That way, you will not owe late fees or other charges.
- Keep the money you are saving separate from the money you spend.
- Consider opening a savings account in a bank or credit union.
- If you keep cash at home, keep the money you are saving separate from your spending money. Keep all your cash someplace safe.

Table 13.1. Minimizing the Expenses and Increasing the Savings

What You Did Not Buy This Month	**Money Saved**
Music downloads	$5.00
Shirt	$30.00
Movie ticket	$10.00
Top off gas tank	$15.00
Cups of coffee	$12.00
What You Saved This Month	**$72.00**

CHAPTER 14

WHY SAVINGS MATTERS

About This Chapter: Text in this chapter begins with excerpts from "Why Savings Matters: The Latest Research," Consumer Financial Protection Bureau (CFPB), May 17, 2020; Text under the heading "It is Never Too Early – or Too Late – to Save" is excerpted from "It's Never Too Early – or Too Late – to Save," Federal Trade Commission (FTC), August 28, 2014.

Research suggests that saving for emergencies is the first line of defense against unexpected expenses, such as car repairs, a medical bill, or even a broken phone.

The Importance of Savings

For millions of Americans, establishing a savings fund for emergencies is the first step to improving their overall financial well-being and staying on track to reaching their financial goals.

Financial emergencies can happen to anyone. Research suggests that even individuals with a reasonable ability to save find it hard to recover unless they have access to savings they can use for these expenses.

Putting money away into savings – even in small amounts – can help people feel more confident in their ability to overcome a financial shock. Saving just one month of expenses can help protect many households from unexpected emergencies or experiencing significant financial hardship.

Without a dedicated savings fund for emergencies, these unplanned costs may become credit card or loan debt that is harder to pay off. Similarly, individuals may pull from other savings intended for longer-term security, like retirement.

What Research Tells Us

Research suggests that the lack of savings can set Americans back and make it difficult to recover financially or protect against future financial shocks.

- Nonsavers indicate greater reliance on high-cost financial services, such as pawn or payday loans.

Other Reasons to Save

- It is important to save for periodic expenses – those that come only once or a few times a year such as renter's insurance, income taxes, automobile insurance, and children's school supplies. While not unexpected, they can still surprise you.
- Saving money is particularly important for people whose income fluctuates, or varies. An hourly worker who is not guaranteed a fixed number of hours per week has fluctuating income. Someone who is employed seasonally – receiving income for only eight out of twelve months because work stops – has fluctuating income, too.

(Source: "A Financial Empowerment Toolkit for Community Volunteers," Consumer Financial Protection Bureau (CFPB).)

- 71 percent of households face difficulty saving because of expenses they did not plan for.
- More than half of households struggle to make ends meet after their most expensive financial shocks.

It Is Never Too Early – or Too Late – to Save

No matter your stage of life, it is important to have savings: Whether it is for a special purchase, a college education, your first home, retirement, or an emergency fund.

But, just how do you get started and stay on course? Here are a few tips and resources to help you reach your savings goal.

Create a budget. The first step toward taking control of your financial life is to evaluate how much money you take in and how much money you spend. Start by listing your income from all sources. Then, list your "fixed" expenses – those that are the same each month – such as rent, car payments, and insurance premiums. Next, list the expenses that vary – such as entertainment, recreation, and clothing. Writing down all your expenses, even those that seem insignificant, is a helpful way to track your spending patterns, identify necessary expenses, and prioritize the rest. Use our budget worksheet to get started.

Pay yourself first. This phrase refers to the practice of automatically making a savings contribution or investment with your income before it can reach your wallet. For example, consider a payroll savings plan where a certain amount goes directly into your savings account each payday. This can help you get used to managing living expenses with what looks like a smaller paycheck, when actually you are building up your own savings.

Get to know the value of compound interest. Setting aside money and watching it grow can be a powerful motivator. Compound interest can be thought of as "interest on interest." It is the interest you earn on your initial investment plus all the interest that has accumulated over time. It makes your investment grow at a faster rate than simple interest, which is interest earned only on your original investment.

Watch your money double with the Rule of 72. The Rule of 72 is an easy way to calculate how long it will take for your investment to double at a given interest rate if you do not make any further deposits. Take the number 72 and divide it by the interest rate you hope to earn. That number gives you the approximate number of years it will take for your investment to double. For example, say you invest $8,000 in a mutual fund with an average 8 percent rate of return. In about 9 years (72 divided by 8) your savings will have doubled to $16,000.

Keep it going. If you get a raise at work, bank it. If you pay off your car, bank the monthly payments. If you are not sure you will remember to make the deposits, consider automated transfers from your checking account to your savings or investment account. That way you never even notice it. If you were able to live on less before, you can continue to.

Get creative. Save and have fun. Saving money does not have to be boring or a chore. Get your hair done for free or at a discount by searching online for local beauty schools and making an appointment with a student in training. Pack your lunch. Did you know that spending $6 a day on lunch means spending about $800 a year? Instead of buying books, music, and DVDs, dust off your library card or trade favorite reads, music, and movies with friends. Go generic on your favorite grocery, beauty and healthcare items. Keep your car tires properly inflated, which can increase fuel efficiency, meaning less money spent on gas. The list is endless.

Bottom-line: Everyone has the ability to save. You can start small and save only $10 a week or month. Over time, your deposits will add up. Even small amounts of savings can help you in the future.

CHAPTER 15
BANKING BASICS

About This Chapter: "Banking Basics," © 2017 Omnigraphics.

Many parents set up bank savings accounts for their children as soon as they are born, so it is possible that you have been dealing with banks for many years. But, perhaps you have never done business with a bank, or if you had an account as a child maybe you are ready to transition to a more adult account of your own. In any case, it pays to learn a bit about the banking system so you can understand your choices and make informed decisions.

What Is a Bank?

It may seem obvious, but a bank is more than the building on the corner with a drive-through cash machine. Odds are that building houses a branch of a much larger organization that consists of many branches and an overarching corporate structure. In some cases there may be no brick-and-mortar building at all. Some banks strictly operate online, with all transactions taking place via a secure website.

Whatever its structure, a bank is a financial institution that provides a wide variety of functions for businesses and individual customers. But, its main purpose is to take in funds, pool them together, and use that money for loans and other investments. The money it earns is then paid to depositors in the form of interest.

Bank Services

Most of the many functions performed by banks probably will not concern you at the moment, but it is worthwhile to understand a few of the more common services they provide, including:

- **Savings accounts.** There are simple savings accounts that pay a relatively small amount of interest on your deposits but allow you to withdraw your money at any time. Then there are other types of accounts that earn a higher rate of interest in exchange for leaving your money in the bank for longer periods, such as money market accounts and certificates of deposit (CDs).

- **Checking accounts.** When you open a checking account you deposit funds and receive a book of checks, slips of paper that are a promise to pay a specified amount of money from your account. These days, writing physical checks is becoming something of a rarity, but checking accounts also let you make deposits and withdrawals from an ATM (automated teller machine), pay bills online, and transfer money between accounts.
- **Debit cards.** When you open a savings or checking account, the bank might issue a debit card to you. This card has a magnetic strip and an embedded microchip that can be scanned by readers at ATMs, restaurants, gas stations, and stores, allowing you to conduct transactions using funds in your accounts at the bank.
- **Loans.** One of the primary ways banks make money is by taking funds it receives from depositors and lending it to people who need it. The bank makes money by charging a higher fee for these loans than it pays out in interest.
- **Credit cards.** Credit cards are, essentially, a type of loan. Unlike with a debit card, money for credit-card purchases does not automatically come out of the customer's bank account. Rather, the bank is advancing the funds to a merchant or other payee with the understanding that the customer will pay the money back to the bank.
- **Online and mobile banking.** When you open an account, you are typically given a user ID and password to get access to the bank's secure website. Then, from any computer with an Internet connection, you can check your balances, transfer funds between accounts, and pay bills. Most banks now also have mobile apps that allow you to perform these same functions from your phone or tablet.

Advantages of Banks

As an informed consumer, it is to your benefit to learn how banks can work for you. Some advantages include:

- **You earn money.** Funds you deposit into a savings account – and some checking accounts – earn interest, which the bank pays you for letting it use your money. Generally, the interest earned on these accounts is not a lot, but it is more than you would get by keeping it in a drawer.
- **Your money is safe.** The Federal Deposit Insurance Corporation (FDIC), an independent agency created by the U.S. Congress, insures most personal bank deposits up to $250,000. There are some types of bank investments that are not covered, but customers with regular savings and checking accounts know their money is guaranteed to be there.

- **Banks help you budget.** A bank statement, either mailed to you monthly or accessed online, lets you keep track of income and expenses very easily. You can also set up different accounts for different purposes. For example, you might have one savings account where you accumulate money for a car and another for short-term use, such as school expenses.
- **Convenience.** Banks give you option of buying goods and services or paying bills as easily as possible using their various payment methods, including debit cards and online or mobile banking. They also allow you to go to the bank location to make deposits or withdrawals or take advantage of the nearest ATM to perform the same functions.

Bank Fees

Unsurprisingly, banks charge fees for many of their services. These vary depending on the bank and the type of account, so it is smart to shop around. Some bank fees can include:

- **Checking account fees.** Most banks charge a monthly fee for maintaining your checking account, usually between $10 and $20. This can often be avoided by either keeping a minimum balance in that account or by maintaining a minimum balance in a saving account at the same bank.
- **Overdraft charge.** If you use more money than you have in your checking account – either by writing a check or by using your debit card – and the bank covers the difference, you may be charged an overdraft fee of $20 to $40.
- **Returned check fee.** A returned check fee is incurred when you write a check without enough money in your account and the bank does not cover the difference. The bank may charge as much as $40 in such a case.
- **ATM fees.** Usually banks do not charge customers for using their own cash machines. But, if you use an ATM operated by another bank, the other bank will charge a fee, and in some instances your own bank may add a fee, as well. The average charge is around $3.

Other bank charges can include foreign transaction fees; paper statement fees, charged by some banks if you want hard-copies mailed to you; inactivity fees, which are sometimes incurred if an account lies dormant for a long time; check-printing fees; and lost debit-card fees.

Choosing a Bank

As with shopping for clothes, a car, or anything else, when selecting a bank it is smart to shop around. Banks vary considerably in areas such as the fees they charge, the amount of interest they pay, and the services they offer, and some are bound to meet your needs better than others. Some factors to consider:

- **Fees.** One of the most important things to learn is how much it is going to cost you to do business with a bank. Ask about account maintenance charges, ATM fees, overdraft fees, and any other charges that may be associated with the accounts you plan to open.
- **Legitimacy.** You want to be sure you are dealing with a reliable, established bank. One of the most important things is to be sure the bank is a member of the FDIC. The bank's website will usually tell you this, but you can also go to FDIC.gov and search their Bank Find tool just to be sure.
- **Location.** Even people who do not actually go to the bank building very often tend to select a bank near where they live or work. If the need arises for a personal visit, you will appreciate the convenience.
- **Size.** If you travel a lot it could be helpful to do business with a large bank that has branches in several states, or even outside the country.
- **Minimum deposit amount.** Many banks have a minimum amount required to open an account, and this can vary widely.
- **Types of services offered.** Right now, you might only be interested in opening a savings account, but at some point you may want a checking account, credit card, or car loan. It is good to know your options before you begin doing business with a bank.
- **Technology.** If you plan to make regular use of electronic banking, be sure the bank offers what you need. Ask about online fund transfers, remote deposits, text and e-mail alerts for unusual account activity, and mobile apps.

Finally, when shopping for a bank, use the Internet to your advantage. You can learn a lot about a bank from its website. There you will find information about interest rates, fees, services they offer, and special promotions they may be running (such as free check-printing for new customers). And, as with pretty much everything these days, you can Google the bank's name and find useful customer reviews and ratings.

References

1. "Banking 101," USTrust.com, 2016.
2. "Banking Basics," Indiana Department of Financial Institutions, n.d.
3. "Banking Basics 101: A Quick Lesson in Banking and Saving," CesiSolutions.org, September 21, 2013.
4. Calonia, Jennifer. "Banking," Learnvest.com, June 1, 2012.
5. Campisi, Natalie. "Banking 101 Guide: Tips and Terms to Know before Opening Your First Account," GoBankingRates.com, August 19, 2016.
6. "Selecting a Bank," Teensguidetomoney.com, n.d.

CHAPTER 16
SETTING UP A SAVINGS ACCOUNT

It is never too early to start saving and managing your money. The earlier you start saving, the better it is for your financial future. There are wide options to invest in, and the most basic and reliable investment option is to open a savings account. A savings account is a great asset, especially during an unprecedented emergency. A standard savings account is a type of account offered by all banking and financial institutions that let customers deposit their money, withdraw money as and when they require, and earn interest on their deposit amounts. Most banks and financial institutions have transaction limits, and require the account holder to maintain a minimum balance. Bank deposits are insured with the Federal Deposit Insurance Corporation (FDIC) to safeguard customer's money if a bank goes through a financial crisis. Money can be withdrawn, deposited, or transferred from the savings account through an automated teller machine (ATM), a direct deposit, or an electronic transfer.

Things to Consider before Opening a Savings Account

While thinking of choosing the type of savings account, it may help to keep certain points in mind such as:

- **The purpose of the account.** Having an idea of what the money will be used for can help decide which account to settle on. A savings account is helpful for short-term financial goals such as an emergency fund, a vacation, or a sizable upcoming purchase.
- **Initial deposit requirements.** Some savings accounts require an opening deposit, and some others do not. Depending on the availability of finances, one can choose a bank and their account options accordingly.
- **Account-linked fees and insurance.** Garner as much information regarding the bank's insurance provision for the respective account, the account's maintenance fee, and excessive withdrawal and transfer fees.

- **Minimum balance.** Some accounts require a minimum balance to be retained in the account so as to earn the annual percentage yield (APY) assigned to the account. This is known as a "minimum balance requirement" failing which the account holder may incur a penalty that must be avoided.
- **The assigned annual percentage yield (APY) for the account.** An APY is the amount paid to the account holder as interest, which is always represented as a percentage. When deciding between different types of savings accounts, keep the APY in mind. A higher interest rate can seem impressive but keep your finances in mind before deciding on the account.

Opening a Savings Account

Before deciding on a savings account, it may help to know the different kinds of savings accounts available such as:

- **Regular savings account.** These accounts are great for short- or long-term investments, and offer a basic interest rate. They are offered by banks and credit unions. You can earn an interest on these accounts.
- **High-yield savings account.** These accounts offer a higher interest rate and are suitable for customers who require online banking services.
- **Money market accounts.** For customers who wish to access their money regularly, this can be the best option as it combines the features of a savings and checking account. This type of account is offered by traditional and online banks.
- **Certificate of deposit account.** This type is a time deposit account and is the best option for long-term saving where the account holder deposits a certain amount for a specified time period (between 30 days and 5 years) and simultaneously earns an interest. Post maturity, the amount can be withdrawn or deposited again.
- **Cash management account.** This account helps save money that may later be invested in retirement accounts or taxable brokerages. Online brokerage companies offer their customers this type of service to investors. The money stored often earns a higher interest.
- **Specialty savings accounts.** As the name suggests, these accounts are for special purposes in the near or distant future. Some examples include student savings accounts, Christmas club savings accounts, kids' savings accounts, and health savings accounts.

After considerable research and settling on the type of account most suited to your financial needs, it is important to assemble all the required documentation that may be asked of the customer. Though different banks have minor differences in the documents and official paperwork that they require for a successful account opening process, in general, U.S. citizens will have to visit a branch or apply online if the bank offers it, and provide a name, address, a valid telephone number, a government issued photo identification document, and a Social Security number (SSN) to the bank upon request.

For nonresidents, or immigrants, the required documentation includes U.S.-based address proof, and local contact information, a valid U.S. passport and driver's license, an initial deposit, and proof of immigration.

Once the documents are ready, you can also contact the financial institution's customer service to find out if they still need further documentation or anything else that may make your account opening process easier.

The next set of steps to follow while opening a new savings account are:

- **Weigh the options.** Undertake extensive research and compare different banks and credit unions to find the most reasonable interest rates and account types before applying for an account.
- **Apply.** There are options to apply for a savings account, such as visiting the branch in person, applying online, over the phone, or by mailing in your application. Depending on your convenience choose the best one and start your savings account application process.
- **Provide your Social Security number.** This information is crucial as the interest you earn in the savings account is taxable. The customer may also be asked for their taxpayer identification number for verification purposes.
- **Give relevant contact information.** When asked in the application form or by banking representatives, provide accurate contact information such as your residence address, phone number, e-mail address, and your full name as it appears on official records.
- **Choose a specific type of account.** If you plan to open a savings account individually, or a joint account, make sure to give these details clearly in the application and let the bank know the same.
- **Peruse the terms and conditions.** The bank will provide you with important information such as legal liabilities, account details, interest charges, disclosure fees, and documentation at the end of the application form. Before signing the form, make sure to read it thoroughly. Contact the bank to clarify or modify any details provided.
- **Start with an opening deposit.** Some may require an opening deposit depending on your financial institution and account, whereas others will not. Either way, it is beneficial to deposit a particular amount to enable interest earnings at the earliest. One can even transfer money from an existing account or by check.
- **Submit the application.** Once the application form is submitted successfully, either online or in-person, you can expect a minimum gap of 5 business days for the account to be active and ready for use. In the

Making Savings Automatic

If you have a bank account, you can arrange to have some of the deposited money moved automatically to a savings account. If your weekly paycheck of $245 is directly deposited into your checking account every week, you can have $10 automatically transferred into a savings account. Once you set this system up, you may forget about that $10. And by the end of the year, you will have over $500 in that account.

(Source: "A Financial Empowerment Toolkit for Community Volunteers," Consumer Financial Protection Bureau (CFPB).)

meantime, you may be contacted by bank representatives for verification. Once you receive an official confirmation from the bank, you can start with direct deposits and transfers into the account. The bank or financial institution will provide you with the debit card, checkbook, and a welcome kit, if applicable, with the guidelines and account details to help you start using your account without any issue.

Deposits and Withdrawals

Once the savings account is ready for use, you can start depositing money through means such as:

- Direct transfers from checking accounts once they are linked and set up for regular deposits
- Depositing cash or checks by visiting the branch, or at an ATM
- Electronic transfers
- Direct deposits

To access the money in the savings account, you can do so by:

- Requesting a check from the bank
- Making electronic transfers
- Transferring money to a checking account
- Withdrawing funds from an ATM or at the bank from a teller

Setting up a savings account is beneficial and completely safe. It can help grow your finances with little effort and is a financial asset for the future. Choose the bank and the account that best suits your financial goals, resources, and needs.

References

1. Kagan, Julia. "Savings Accounts," Investopedia, March 19, 2021.
2. Burnette, Margarette. "How to Open a Savings Account: Step by Step," NerdWallet, April 30, 2021.

3. Napoletano, E. "7 Questions to Ask before Opening a Savings Account," *Forbes,* December 29, 2020.
4. Pritchard, Justin. "What Is a Savings Account?" The Balance, April 24, 2021.
5. Loncar, Zorica. "How to Open a Bank Account in the USA," Wise, December 12, 2020.
6. Lake, Rebecca. "6 Types of Savings Accounts," *Forbes,* September 24, 2020.

CHAPTER 17
BASICS OF INVESTING

About This Chapter: Text under the heading "The Differences between Saving and Investing" is excerpted from "Saving and Investing for Students," U.S. Securities and Exchange Commission (SEC), October 17, 2010; Text under the heading "What Kinds of Investment Products Are There?" is excerpted from "Introduction to Investing," Inverstor.gov, U.S. Securities and Exchange Commission (SEC), August 25, 2016; Text under the heading "The Magic of Compounding" is excerpted from "The Magic of Compounding," U.S. Department of Labor (DOL), February 1, 2001.

The Differences between Saving and Investing

Saving

Your "savings" are usually put into the safest places, or products, that allow you access to your money at any time. Savings products include savings accounts, checking accounts, and certificates of deposit. Some deposits in these products may be insured by the Federal Deposit Insurance Corporation or the National Credit Union Administration. But, there is a tradeoff for security and ready availability. Your money is paid a low wage as it works for you.

After paying off credit cards or other high interest debt, most smart investors put enough money in a savings product to cover an emergency, like sudden unemployment. Some make sure they have up to six months of their income in savings so that they know it will absolutely be there for them when they need it.

But, how "safe" is a savings account if you leave all of your money there for a long time, and the interest it earns does not keep up with inflation? What if you save a dollar when it can buy a loaf of bread. But, years later when you withdraw that dollar plus the interest you earned on it, it can only buy half a loaf? This is why many people put some of their money in savings, but look to investing so they can earn more over long periods of time, say three years or longer.

Table 17.1. Basic Types of Products

Savings	Investments
Savings accounts	Bonds
Certificates of deposit	Stocks
Checking accounts	Mutual funds, exchange-traded funds
	Real estate
	Commodities (gold, silver, etc.)

Investing

When you "invest," you have a greater chance of losing your money than when you "save." The money you invest in securities, mutual funds, and other similar investments typically is not federally insured. You could lose your "principal" – the amount you have invested. But, you also have the opportunity to earn more money.

What Kinds of Investment Products Are There?

Stocks

Stocks are a type of security that gives stockholders a share of ownership in a company. Stocks also are called "equities."

Bonds

A bond is a debt security, similar to an IOU. Borrowers issue bonds to raise money from investors willing to lend them money for a certain amount of time.

When you buy a bond, you are lending to the issuer, which may be a government, municipality, or corporation. In return, the issuer promises to pay you a specified rate of interest during the life of the bond and to repay the principal, also known as "face value" or "par value of the bond," when it "matures," or comes due after a set period of time.

Municipal Bonds

Municipal bonds (or "munis" for short) are debt securities issued by states, cities, counties and other governmental entities to fund day-to-day obligations and to finance capital projects such as building schools, highways or sewer systems. By purchasing municipal bonds, you are in effect lending money to the bond issuer in exchange for a promise of regular interest payments, usually semi-annually, and the return of the original investment, or "principal." A municipal bond's maturity date (the date when the issuer of the bond repays the principal) may be years in the future. Short-term bonds mature in one to three years, while long-term bonds would not mature for more than a decade.

Mutual Funds

A mutual fund is a company that pools money from many investors and invests the money in securities such as stocks, bonds, and short-term debt. The combined holdings of the mutual fund are known as its "portfolio." Investors buy shares in mutual funds. Each share represents an investor's part ownership in the fund and the income it generates.

Exchange-Traded Funds

ETFs are a type of exchange-traded investment product that must register with the SEC under the 1940 Act as either an open-end investment company (generally known as "funds") or a unit investment trust.

Annuities

An annuity is a contract between you and an insurance company that requires the insurer to make payments to you, either immediately or in the future. You buy an annuity by making either a single payment or a series of payments. Similarly, your payout may come either as one lump-sum payment or as a series of payments over time.

Certificates of Deposit

A certificate of deposit (CD) is a savings account that holds a fixed amount of money for a fixed period of time, such as six months, one year, or five years, and in exchange, the issuing bank pays interest. When you cash in or redeem your CD, you receive the money you originally invested plus any interest. Certificates of deposit are considered to be one of the safest savings options. A CD bought through a federally insured bank is insured up to $250,000. The $250,000 insurance covers all accounts in your name at the same bank, not each CD or account you have at the bank.

Money Market Funds

Money market funds are a type of mutual fund developed in the 1970s as an option for investors to purchase a pool of securities that generally provided higher returns than interest-bearing bank accounts. They have grown significantly in the ensuing decades.

Commodities

Commodity futures contracts are an agreement to buy or sell a specific quantity of a commodity at a specified price on a particular date in the future. Metals, grains, and other food, as well as financial instruments, including U.S. and foreign currencies, are traded in the futures market. With limited exceptions, trading in futures contracts must be executed on the floor of a commodity exchange. Exchange-traded commodity futures and options provide traders with contracts of a set unit size, a fixed expiration date, and centralized clearing. In centralized clearing, a clearing corporation acts as

How to Avoid Problems with Investments

Choosing someone to help you with your investments is one of the most important investment decisions you will ever make. While most investment professionals are honest and hardworking, you must watch out for those few unscrupulous individuals. They can make your life's savings disappear in an instant.

Be wary of promises of quick profits, offers to share "inside information," and pressure to invest before you have an opportunity to investigate. These are all warning signs of fraud. Ask your investment professional for written materials and prospectuses, and read them before you invest.

a single counterparty to every transaction and guarantees the completion and credit worthiness of all transactions.

Hedge Funds

Hedge funds pool money from investors and invest in securities or other types of investments with the goal of getting positive returns. Hedge funds are not regulated as heavily as mutual funds and generally have more leeway than mutual funds to pursue investments and strategies that may increase the risk of investment losses. Hedge funds are limited to wealthier investors who can afford the higher fees and risks of hedge fund investing, and institutional investors, including pension funds.

Real Estate Investment Trusts

Real estate investment trusts ("REITs") allow individuals to invest in large-scale, income-producing real estate. A REIT is a company that owns and typically operates income-producing real estate or related assets. These may include office buildings, shopping malls, apartments, hotels, resorts, self-storage facilities, warehouses, and mortgages or loans. Unlike other real estate companies, a REIT does not develop real estate properties to resell them. Instead, a REIT buys and develops properties primarily to operate them as part of its own investment portfolio.

International Investing

Two of the chief reasons why people invest in international investments and investments with international exposure are:

- **Diversification.** International investing may help U.S. investors to spread their investment risk among foreign companies and markets in addition to U.S. companies and markets.
- **Growth.** International investing takes advantage of the potential for growth in some foreign economies, particularly in emerging markets.

The Magic of Compounding

Compounding investment earnings is what can make even small investments become large investments given enough time.

Table 17.2. Rates of Return over Time

Years	4%	6%	8%	10%
10	$1,481	$1,791	$2,159	$2,994
20	$2,191	$3,207	$4,661	$6,728
30	$3,243	$5,743	$10,063	$17,449

How it works. The money you save (either in a savings account, a mutual funds or in individual stocks) earns interest. Then you earn interest on the money you originally save, plus on the interest you have accumulated. As your savings grow, you earn interest on a bigger and bigger pool of money.

For example, the value of $1000 compounded at various rates of return over time is shown in the following chart.

Start saving early. For every 10 years you delay before starting to save for retirement, you will need to save three times as much each month to catch up.

Starting at 20. If you put $1,000 a year into an IRA every year from age 20 through age 30 (for 11 years) and stop – and the account earns seven percent annually – your savings will equal $168,514 at age 65.

Starting at age 30. If you do not start until age 30, but save the same $1,000 amount annually, but for 35 years straight at the same seven percent rate, you will have saved three times as much money, but your account will grow to only $147,913 at age 65.

From the Employee Benefits Security Administration's publication Savings Fitness: A Guide to Your Money and Your Financial Future, available to consumers by calling 866-444-3272, and the Certified Financial Planner Board of Standards.

CHAPTER 18
UNDERSTANDING STOCK MARKETS

About This Chapter: Text beginning with the heading "What Are Stocks?" is excerpted from "Stocks," Inverstor.gov, U.S. Securities and Exchange Commission (SEC), March 7, 2011; Text beginning with the heading "Public Companies" is excerpted from "How Stock Markets Work," Inverstor.gov, U.S. Securities and Exchange Commission (SEC), May 9, 2013.

What Are Stocks?

Stocks are a type of security that gives stockholders a share of ownership in a company. Stocks also are called "equities."

Why Do People Buy Stocks?

Investors buy stocks for various reasons. Here are some of them:

- Capital appreciation, which occurs when a stock rises in price
- Dividend payments, which come when the company distributes some of its earnings to stockholders
- Ability to vote shares and influence the company

Why Do Companies Issue Stock?

Companies issue stock to get money for various things, which may include:

- Paying off debt
- Launching new products
- Expanding into new markets or regions
- Enlarging facilities or building new ones

What Kinds of Stock Are There?

There are two main kinds of stocks, common stock and preferred stock.

- Common stock entitles owners to vote at shareholder meetings and receive dividends.

- Preferred stockholders usually do not have voting rights but they receive dividend payments before common stockholders do, and have priority over common stockholders if the company goes bankrupt and its assets are liquidated.

Common and preferred stocks may fall into one or more of the following categories:

- Growth stocks have earnings growing at a faster rate than the market average. They rarely pay dividends and investors buy them in the hope of capital appreciation. A start-up technology company is likely to be a growth stock.
- Income stocks pay dividends consistently. Investors buy them for the income they generate. An established utility company is likely to be an income stock.
- Value stocks have a low price-to-earnings (PE) ratio, meaning they are cheaper to buy than stocks with a higher PE. Value stocks may be growth or income stocks, and their low PE ratio may reflect the fact that they have fallen out of favor with investors for some reason. People buy value stocks in the hope that the market has overreacted and that the stock's price will rebound.
- Blue-chip stocks are shares in large, well-known companies with a solid history of growth. They generally pay dividends.

Another way to categorize stocks is by the size of the company, as shown in its market capitalization. There are large-cap, mid-cap, and small-cap stocks. Shares in very small companies are sometimes called "microcap stocks." The very lowest priced stocks are known as "penny stocks." These companies may have little or no earnings. Penny stocks do not pay dividends and are highly speculative.

What Are the Benefits and Risks of Stocks?

Stocks offer investors the greatest potential for growth (capital appreciation) over the long haul. Investors willing to stick with stocks over long periods of time, say 15 years, generally have been rewarded with strong, positive returns.

But, stock prices move down as well as up. There is no guarantee that the company whose stock you hold will grow and do well, so you can lose money you invest in stocks.

If a company goes bankrupt and its assets are liquidated, common stockholders are the last in line to share in the proceeds. The company's bondholders will be paid first, then holders of preferred stock. If you are a common stockholder, you get whatever is left, which may be nothing.

Even when companies are not in danger of failing, their stock price may fluctuate up or down. Large company stocks as a group, for example, have lost money on average about one out of every three years. If you have to sell shares on a day when the stock price is below the price you paid for the shares, you will lose money on the sale.

Market fluctuations can be unnerving to some investors. A stock's price can be affected by factors inside the company, such as a faulty product, or by events the company has no control over, such as political or market events.

Stocks usually are one part of an investor's holdings. If you are young and saving for a long-term goal such as retirement, you may want to hold more stocks than bonds. Investors nearing or in retirement may want to hold more bonds than stocks.

The risks of stock holdings can be offset in part by investing in a number of different stocks. Investing in other kinds of assets that are not stocks, such as bonds, is another way to offset some of the risks of owning stocks.

How to Buy and Sell Stocks

You can buy and sell stocks through:

Direct stock plans. Some companies allow you to buy or sell their stock directly through them without using a broker. This saves on commissions, but you may have to pay other fees to the plan, including if you transfer shares to a broker to sell them. Some companies limit direct stock plans to employees of the company or existing shareholders. Some require minimum amounts for purchases or account levels.

Direct stock plans usually will not allow you to buy or sell shares at a specific market price or at a specific time. Instead, the company will buy or sell shares for the plan at set times – such as daily, weekly, or monthly – and at an average market price. Depending on the plan, you may be able to automate your purchases and have the cost deducted automatically from your savings account.

Dividend reinvestment plans. These plans allow you to buy more shares of a stock you already own by reinvesting dividend payments into the company. You must sign an agreement with the company to have this done. Check with the company or your brokerage firm to see if you will be charged for this service.

Discount or full-service broker. Brokers buy and sell shares for customers for a fee, known as a "commission."

Stock funds are another way to buy stocks. These are a type of mutual fund that invests primarily in stocks. Depending on its investment objective and policies, a stock fund may concentrate on a particular type of stock, such as blue chips, large-cap value stocks, or mid-cap growth stocks. Stock funds are offered by investment companies and can be purchased directly from them or through a broker or adviser.

Understanding Fees

Buying and selling stocks entails fees. A direct stock plan or a dividend reinvestment plan may charge you a fee for that service. Brokers who buy and sell stocks for you charge a commission. A discount brokerage charges lower commissions than what you would pay at a full-service brokerage. But, generally you have to research and choose investments by yourself. A full-service brokerage costs more, but the higher commissions pay for investment advice based on that firm's research.

Avoiding Fraud

Stocks in public companies are registered with the SEC and in most cases, public companies are required to file reports to the SEC quarterly and annually. Annual reports include financial statements that have been audited by an independent audit firm. Information on public companies can be found on the SEC's EDGAR system.

Public Companies

Public companies are a key part of the American economy. They play a major role in the savings, investment, and retirement plans of many Americans. If you have a pension plan or own a mutual fund, chances are that the plan or mutual fund owns stock in public companies. Like millions of Americans, you may also invest directly in public companies.

What Is a Public Company?

The term "public company" can be defined in various ways. There are two commonly understood ways in which a company is considered public: first, the company's securities trade on public markets; and second, the company discloses certain business and financial information regularly to the public.

In general, we use the term to refer to a company that has public reporting obligations. Companies are subject to public reporting requirements if they:

- Sell securities in a public offering (such as an initial public offering or IPO)
- Allow their investor base to reach a certain size, which triggers public reporting obligations
- Voluntarily register with the U.S. Securities and Exchange Commission (SEC)

A private company also can become subject to public reporting requirements by merging with a public shell company. This process is called a "reverse merger." As with any investment, investors should proceed with caution when considering whether to invest in reverse merger companies.

As mentioned, companies are viewed as public if they are subject to public reporting obligations. There are instances, however, where the securities of a company that does not regularly report business and financial information to the public are nonetheless traded on smaller public markets. Investing in these companies is riskier as there can be little public information to allow investors to make an informed investment decision.

Transparency and Continuing Disclosures

A public company's disclosure obligations begin with the initial registration statement that it files with the SEC. But, the disclosure requirements do not end there.

Public companies must continue to keep their shareholders informed on a regular basis by filing periodic reports and other materials with the SEC. The SEC makes these documents publicly available without charge on its EDGAR website. The filed documents are subject to review by SEC staff for compliance with federal securities laws.

Following are some of the reports that may be filed by U.S.-based public companies. Foreign companies that file reports with the SEC may file different types of reports.

- **Annual reports on Form 10-K.** This report includes the company's audited annual financial statements and a discussion of the company's business results.
- **Quarterly reports on Form 10-Q.** Public companies must file this report for each of the first three quarters of their fiscal year. (After the fourth quarter, public companies file an annual report instead of a quarterly report.) The quarterly report includes unaudited financial statements and information about the company's business and results for the previous three months and for the year to date. The quarterly report compares the company's performance in the current quarter and year to date to the same periods in the previous year.
- **Current reports on Form 8-K.** Companies file this report with the SEC to announce major events that shareholders should know about, including bankruptcy proceedings, a change in corporate leadership (such as a new director or high-level officer), and preliminary earnings announcements.
- **Proxy statements.** Shareholder voting constitutes one of the key rights of shareholders. They may elect members of the board of directors, cast nonbinding votes on executive compensation, approve or reject proposed mergers and acquisitions, or vote on other important topics. Proxy statements describe the matters to be voted upon and often disclose information on the company's executive compensation policies and practices.
- **Additional disclosures.** Other federal securities laws and SEC rules require disclosures about a variety of events affecting the company. These include proposed mergers, acquisitions and tender offers; securities transactions by company insiders, and beneficial ownership by a person or group that reaches or exceeds five percent of the company's outstanding shares.

Public Disclosures Protect Investors

Our federal securities laws are based on public disclosure by companies of meaningful business, financial and other information. Public disclosure by companies serves to advance the mission of the SEC.

Market Participants

Part of the mission of the SEC is "to maintain standards for fair, orderly, and efficient markets." To do this, the SEC regulates a number of securities market participants. These include:

- Broker-dealers charge a fee to handle trades between the buyers and sellers of securities. A broker-dealer may buy securities from their customer who is selling or sell from their own inventory to its customer who is buying.
- Clearing agencies are self-regulatory organizations (SROs) that are required to register with the SEC. Like all SROs, they are responsible for writing and enforcing their rules and disciplining members. There are two types of clearing agencies – clearing corporations and depositories.
  - Clearing corporations, such as the National Securities Clearing Corporation (NSCC) and the Fixed Income Clearing Corporation (FICC), compare member transactions, clear those trades and prepare instructions for automated settlement of those trades. Clearing corporations often act as intermediaries in making securities settlements.
  - Depositories, namely The Depository Trust Company (DTC), hold securities certificates for their participants, transfer positions between participants, and maintain ownership records.
- Credit rating agencies provide opinions on the creditworthiness of a company or security. They indicate the credit quality by means of a grade. Generally, credit ratings distinguish between investment grade and noninvestment grade. For example, a credit rating agency may assign a "triple A" credit rating as its top "investment grade" rating, and a "double B" credit rating or below for "noninvestment grade" or "high-yield" corporate bonds. Credit rating agencies registered as such with the SEC are known as "Nationally Recognized Statistical Rating Organizations."
- Electronic Communications Networks, or ECNs, are electronic trading systems that automatically match buy and sell orders at specified prices for users of the system. ECNs register with the SEC as broker-dealers and are subject to Regulation ATS. ATSs are Alternative Trading Systems. This term encompasses all systems that perform securities exchange functions and are not registered with the Commission as exchanges.
- Investment advisers are persons or firms that are in the business of providing investment advice to investors or issuing reports or analyses regarding securities. They do these activities for compensation.
- Securities exchanges are markets where securities are bought and sold. Currently, there are fifteen securities exchanges registered with the SEC as national securities exchanges, including NYSE Euronext, NASDAQ,

The Chicago Board Options Exchange, and BATS Exchange. Securities Exchanges are also SROs.

- A self-regulatory organization (SRO) manages its industry through the adoption of rules governing the conduct of its members. SROs also enforce the rules they adopt and discipline members for violating SRO rules. Two well-known SROs are the Financial Industry Regulatory Authority (FINRA) and the Municipal Securities Rulemaking Board (MSRB). FINRA is the largest SRO in the securities industry. It is the frontline regulator of broker-dealers. MSRB makes rules regulating dealers of municipal securities. The SEC oversees both FINRA and the MSRB. Other SROs include clearing agencies and securities exchanges.
- Transfer agents record changes of security ownership, maintain the issuer's security holder records, cancel and issue certificates, and distribute dividends. Transfer agents stand between issuing companies and security holders. Transfer agents are required to be registered with the SEC, or if the transfer agent is a bank, with a bank regulatory agency. There is no SRO that governs transfer agents. The SEC has announced rules and regulations for all registered transfer agents. The intent is to facilitate the prompt and accurate clearance and settlement of securities transactions and assure the safeguarding of securities and funds.

Types of Orders

The most common types of orders are market orders, limit orders, and stop-loss orders.

- A market order is an order to buy or sell a security immediately. This type of order guarantees that the order will be executed, but does not guarantee the execution price. A market order generally will execute at or near the current bid (for a sell order) or ask (for a buy order) price. However, it is important for investors to remember that the last-traded price is not necessarily the price at which a market order will be executed.
- A limit order is an order to buy or sell a security at a specific price or better. A buy limit order can only be executed at the limit price or lower, and a sell limit order can only be executed at the limit price or higher. Example: An investor wants to purchase shares of ABC stock for no more than $10. The investor could submit a limit order for this amount and this order will only execute if the price of ABC stock is $10 or lower.
- A stop order, also referred to as a stop-loss order is an order to buy or sell a stock once the price of the stock reaches the specified price, known as the "stop price." When the stop price is reached, a stop order becomes a market order.
- A buy stop order is entered at a stop price above the current market price. Investors generally use a buy stop order to limit a loss or protect a profit on

Short Sales

A short sale is the sale of a stock that an investor does not own or a sale which is consummated by the delivery of a stock borrowed by, or for the account of, the investor. Short sales are normally settled by the delivery of a security borrowed by or on behalf of the investor. The investor later closes out the position by returning the borrowed security to the stock lender, typically by purchasing securities on the open market.

Investors who sell stock short typically believe the price of the stock will fall and hope to buy the stock at the lower price and make a profit. Short selling is also used by market makers and others to provide liquidity in response to unanticipated demand, or to hedge the risk of an economic long position in the same security or in a related security. If the price of the stock rises, short sellers who buy it at the higher price will incur a loss.

Brokerage firms typically lend stock to customers who engage in short sales, using the firm's own inventory, the margin account of another of the firm's customers, or another lender. As with buying stock on margin, short sellers are subject to the margin rules and other fees and charges may apply (including interest on the stock loan). If the borrowed stock pays a dividend, the short seller is responsible for paying the dividend to the person or firm making the loan.

a stock that they have sold short. A sell stop order is entered at a stop price below the current market price. Investors generally use a sell stop order to limit a loss or protect a profit on a stock they own.

Types of Brokerage Accounts

A cash account is a type of brokerage account in which the investor must pay the full amount for securities purchased. In a cash account, you are not allowed to borrow funds from your broker to pay for transactions in the account.

A margin account is a type of brokerage account in which your brokerage firm can lend you money to buy securities, with the securities in your portfolio serving as collateral for the loan. As with any other loan, you will incur interest costs when you buy securities on margin.

There are risks involved in purchasing securities on margin. For example, if you buy on margin and the value of your securities declines, your brokerage firm can require you to deposit cash or securities to your account immediately. It can also sell any of the securities in your account to cover any shortfall, without informing you in advance. The brokerage firm decides which of your securities to sell. Even if the brokerage firm notifies you that you have a certain number of days to cover the shortfall, it still may sell your securities before then. A brokerage firm may at any time change the threshold at which customers are subject to a margin call.

Stock Purchases and Sales: Long and Short

Having a "long" position in a security means that you own the security. Investors maintain "long" security positions in the expectation that the stock will rise in value in the future. The opposite of a "long" position is a "short" position.

A "short" position is generally the sale of a stock you do not own. Investors who sell short believe the price of the stock will decrease in value. If the price drops, you can buy the stock at the lower price and make a profit. If the price of the stock rises and you buy it back later at the higher price, you will incur a loss. Short selling is for the experienced investor.

Executing an Order

When you place an order to buy or sell stock, you might not think about where or how your broker will execute the trade. But where and how your order is executed can impact the overall cost of the transaction, including the price you pay for the stock. Here is what you should know about trade execution:

Trade Execution Is Not Instantaneous

Many investors who trade through online brokerage accounts assume they have a direct connection to the securities markets, but they don't. When you push that enter key, your order is sent over the Internet to your broker – who in turn decides which market to send it to for execution. A similar process occurs when you call your broker to place a trade.

While trade execution is usually seamless and quick, it does take time. And prices can change quickly, especially in fast-moving markets. Because price quotes are only for a specific number of shares, investors may not always receive the price they saw on their screen or the price their broker quoted over the phone. By the time your order reaches the market, the price of the stock could be slightly – or very – different.

SEC regulations do not require a trade to be executed within a set period of time. But, if firms advertise their speed of execution, they must not exaggerate or fail to tell investors about the possibility of significant delays.

Your Broker Has Options for Executing Your Trade

Just as you have a choice of brokers, your broker generally has a choice of markets to execute your trade.

- For a stock that is listed on an exchange, your broker may direct the order to that exchange, to another exchange, or to a firm called a "market maker."
- A "market maker" is a firm that stands ready to buy or sell a stock listed on an exchange at publicly quoted prices. As a way to attract orders from brokers, some market makers will pay your broker for routing your order to them – perhaps a penny or more per share. This is called "payment for order flow."
- For a stock that trades in an over-the-counter (OTC) market, your broker may send the order to an "OTC market maker." Many OTC market makers also pay brokers for order flow.

- Your broker may route your order – especially a limit order – to an electronic communications network (ECN) that automatically matches buy and sell orders at specified prices.
- Your broker may decide to send your order to another division of your broker's firm to be filled out of the firm's own inventory. This is called "internalization." In this way, your broker's firm may make money on the "spread" – which is the difference between the price the firm paid for the security and the price at which the firm sells it to you.

Your Broker Has a Duty of "Best Execution"

Many firms use automated systems to handle the orders they receive from their customers. In deciding how to execute orders, your broker has a duty to seek the best execution that is reasonably available for its customers' orders. That means your broker must evaluate the orders it receives from all customers in the aggregate and periodically assess which competing markets, market makers, or ECNs offer the most favorable terms of execution.

The opportunity for "price improvement" is an important factor a broker should consider in executing its customers' orders. "Price improvement" is the opportunity, but not the guarantee, for an order to be executed at a better price than the current quote.

Of course, the additional time it takes some markets to execute orders may result in your getting a worse price than the current quote – especially in a fast-moving market. So, your broker is required to consider whether there is a trade-off between providing its customers' orders with the possibility, but not the guarantee, of better prices and the extra time it may take to do so.

You Have Options for Directing Trades

If for any reason you want to direct your trade to a particular exchange, market maker, or ECN, you may be able to call your broker and ask her or him to do this. But, some brokers may charge for that service. Some brokers offer active traders the ability to direct orders to the market maker or ECN of their choice.

CHAPTER 19
RISKS OF INVESTMENT

About This Chapter: This chapter includes text excerpted from "What Is Risk?" Inverstor.gov, U.S. Securities and Exchange Commission (SEC), March 8, 2012.

All investments involve some degree of risk. In finance, risk refers to the degree of uncertainty and/or potential financial loss inherent in an investment decision. In general, as investment risks rise, investors seek higher returns to compensate themselves for taking such risks.

Every saving and investment product has different risks and returns. Differences include: how readily investors can get their money when they need it, how fast their money will grow, and how safe their money will be.

Business Risk

With a stock, you are purchasing a piece of ownership in a company. With a bond, you are loaning money to a company. Returns from both of these investments require that that the company stays in business. If a company goes bankrupt and its assets are liquidated, common stockholders are the last in line to share in the proceeds. If there are assets, the company's bondholders will be paid first, then holders of preferred stock. If you are a common stockholder, you get whatever is left, which may be nothing.

If you are purchasing an annuity make sure you consider the financial strength of the insurance company issuing the annuity. You want to be sure that the company will still be around, and financially sound, during your payout phase.

Volatility Risk

Even when companies are not in danger of failing, their stock price may fluctuate up or down. Large company stocks as a group, for example, have lost money on average about one out of every three years. Market fluctuations can be unnerving to some investors. A stock's price can be affected by factors inside the company, such as a faulty product, or by events the company has no control over, such as political or market events.

It is often said that the greater the risk, the greater the potential reward in investing, but taking on unnecessary risk is often avoidable. Investors best protect themselves against risk by spreading their money among various investments, hoping that if one investment loses money, the other investments will more than make up for those losses. This strategy, called "diversification," can be neatly summed up as, "Don't put all your eggs in one basket."

(Source: "Saving and Investing for Students," U.S. Securities and Exchange Commission (SEC).)

Inflation Risk

Inflation is a general upward movement of prices. Inflation reduces purchasing power, which is a risk for investors receiving a fixed rate of interest. The principal concern for individuals investing in cash equivalents is that inflation will erode returns.

Interest Rate Risk

Interest rate changes can affect a bond's value. If bonds are held to maturity the investor will receive the face value, plus interest. If sold before maturity, the bond may be worth more or less than the face value. Rising interest rates will make newly issued bonds more appealing to investors because the newer bonds will have a higher rate of interest than older ones. To sell an older bond with a lower interest rate, you might have to sell it at a discount.

Liquidity Risk

This refers to the risk that investors will not find a market for their securities, potentially preventing them from buying or selling when they want. This can be the case with the more complicated investment products. It may also be the case with products that charge a penalty for early withdrawal or liquidation such as a certificate of deposit (CD).

Are There Any Guarantees?

The Federal Deposit Insurance Corporation (FDIC). Savings accounts, insured money market accounts, and certificates of deposit (CDs) are generally viewed as safe because they are federally insured by FDIC. This independent agency of the federal government insures your money up to $250,000 per insured bank. It is important to note that the total is per depositor not per account. But, there is a tradeoff between security and availability; your money earns a low-interest rate.

The FDIC insures deposits only. It does not insure securities, mutual funds, or similar types of investments that banks and thrift institutions may offer.

The National Credit Union Administration (NCUA). The National Credit Union Share Insurance Fund (NCUSIF) is the federal fund created by Congress in 1970 to insure credit union member's deposits in federally insured credit unions. The

Dodd-Frank Act permanently established NCUA's standard maximum share insurance amount at $250,000. NCUSIF is backed by the full faith and credit of the U.S. government.

Securities Investors Protection Corporation (SIPC). Securities you own, including mutual funds that are held for your account by a broker, or a bank's brokerage subsidiary, are not insured against loss in value. The value of your investments can go up or down depending on the demand for them in the market. The Securities Investors Protection Corporation (SIPC), a nongovernment entity, replaces missing stocks and other securities in customer accounts held by SIPC member firm up to $500,000, including up to $250,000 in cash, if the firm fails.

PART 3 | FINANCIAL FUNDAMENTALS

CHAPTER 20

WHAT YOU NEED TO KNOW ABOUT AN INVOICE

An invoice is a document that details the items and services that a company gives to a customer and establishes the customer's responsibility to pay for those items and services.

If products or services were acquired on credit, the invoice generally specifies the conditions of the agreement and lists the various payment options.

Invoices are the business paperwork that allows enterprises to get paid for their services, hence invoicing is critical for small businesses.

Uses of an Invoice

Businesses utilize invoices for several reasons, including:

- To make a payment request to clients in a timely manner
- To keep a watch on sales
- To keep track of their inventory
- To use previous data to anticipate future sales
- To keep track of business income for tax purposes

Contents of an Invoice

An invoice is always presented in a particular format, containing information that allows the seller to clearly set out the terms and conditions of her/his business, to the buyer. The following are the top five items to look for on an invoice:

Vendor Information

Name, firm name, e-mail address, and phone number of the seller should all be prominently displayed. This information is required to determine how and where the payment should be sent. An invoice's processing might be delayed if a ZIP Code or phone number is absent.

Purchase Order Number

When an accounting department receives an invoice with a purchase order number on it, they know that the transaction being invoiced for was previously approved by their own organization.

Now, when the accounting department sees the purchase order number, they can easily open the actual purchase order for reference and double-check that the data on it match those on the invoice.

Invoice Number

An invoice number serves as a reference for the payment that will be made to a vendor. The number is generated by the seller and is included on the invoice.

Both the seller and the client will benefit from an invoice number.

The client can close the purchase order once the invoice is paid. This indicates that the transaction is now complete.

When the vendor receives the check, she or he may look up the invoice number on the pay stub to find out which invoice they were paid for. The invoice can then be marked as paid. This indicates the deal is finished for her or him as well. This system is especially useful for a vendor that does a lot of business with the same client and may have many invoices awaiting clearance and processing.

Pricing and Description

This part informs the customer that the items or services being billed are the same as those previously discussed and that the pricing is as agreed. This information should be a perfect match to the purchase order's (PO) descriptions and pricing.

This is not to say that adjustments are not permitted. For instance, let us imagine a client decides midway through a transaction that he needs 12 instead of 10 of a particular product. Although the discrepancy between the PO and the invoice is visible to the client's accounting department, the invoice is cleared for payment since the discrepancy is not significant and management has signed off on the actual invoice before passing it to accounting.

Terms of Payment

Payment conditions specify when the vendor expects to be paid by the client's accounting department. Terms, such as "payable upon receipt," "net 30 days," "net 45 days," "60," and "90" are frequently used.

Payment terms are frequently a source of misunderstanding since a client's pay period may clash with a vendor's.

Vendors who are dealing with a firm for the first time should make sure that the payment conditions are acceptable to both parties.

Payment conditions are also significant since they inform a client about the payment ways that a vendor accepts. For example, if a merchant accepts PayPal or credit cards as payment methods, the payment terms might include that information.

> **Training individuals in financial management can be an effective way to improve their knowledge in five areas:**
> - Predatory lending practices
> - Public and work-related benefits
> - Banking practices
> - Savings and investing strategies
> - Credit use and interest rates
>
> *(Source: "Facts about Youth Financial Knowledge & Capability," Youth.gov.)*

E-invoicing

People and organizations have found it simpler to rely on electronic invoicing as an alternative to paper since the dawn of the computer era. Electronic invoicing, often known as "e-invoicing," is a type of electronic billing that allows parties to produce, save, and track transaction-related documents to guarantee that the requirements of their agreements are met.

Invoices and receipts, purchase orders, debit and credit notes, payment conditions and instructions, and remittance slips are examples of e-documents. In most cases, digital bills are issued by e-mail, a webpage, or an app. The following are some of the benefits:

- Avoidance of any physical damage to the invoice
- Searching and sorting for certain names, keywords, or dates has never been easier
- Auditability has improved
- The capacity to print or reproduce on-demand, as well as the capacity to collect data and gather business insight
- Paper usage is being reduced

How to Invoice a Client

Vendors should produce and deliver an invoice to their clients as soon as the deal is made and products are being shipped. That way, the details of the job will be fresh in their minds and will be paid as soon as possible. One should also make sure that the invoice has all the information that a customer will need to pay, such as the company name, the invoice due date, and the total amount due.

References

1. Hayes, Adam. "Invoice," Investopedia, October 25, 2020.
2. "What Is an Invoice?" Fresh Books, April 1, 2019.
3. "How to Read an Invoice: The 5 Most Important Things to Look For," Fresh Books, April 14, 2019.

CHAPTER 21
UNDERSTANDING A BANK STATEMENT

About This Chapter: "Understanding a Bank Statement," © 2021 Omnigraphics.

People having a savings or checking account can usually expect a bank statement from their bank or financial institution on a timely basis. Such financial statements may arrive through mail or via online bank accounts.

A bank statement is a document delivered by the bank that summarizes the account holder's entire transactions for a particular period of time, typically a month. Also known as "account statement," this document has details of the account holder's bank, as well as a complete record of deposits and withdrawals made by the account holder, interest gained on the balance, charges incurred, and the opening and closing balances for a period of time. The bank statement may also be requested by a mortgage lender to ensure that a person has adequate money to make monthly payments.

Details of a Bank Statement

Understanding the bank statement may help a person gain a better insight into their spending habits, make smarter financial decisions, and create precise budgets. Though these statements might be confusing at times, they do include a lot of information that is helpful. While certain details may differ from one bank to another, most bank statements will contain the following particulars:

- **Bank information.** The bank's contact information, including their phone number and postal address, will be in the statement.
- **Personal information.** The statement includes the account holder's name and contact information.
- **Transactions.** Cash deposits, cash withdrawals, checks deposited, automated teller machine (ATM) withdrawals, automated clearing house (ACH) transfers, and pending transactions are all examples of a transaction.
- **Charges.** Charges levied for any financial services can be seen in the bank statement.

- **Statement periods.** Certain banks utilize the first and final day of the month, while others utilize certain days of the month to start and end a period of the transaction.
- **Balance details.** Account holders can see where they started and how far they have progressed or regressed throughout the month by looking at their balances.
- **Earned interest.** If the account holder has an interest-bearing account, all interest generated during the statement period will be shown in their statement.

Paper Statement versus Electronic Statement

Most banks provide account holders an option of receiving their bank statements in a variety of formats. A printed statement can be posted to your address, whereas an electronic bank statement can be fed into your account. Logging into your account and looking for a menu option that says "bank statements" is normally necessary to view an electronic bank statement. If a statement option is not seen on the main menu, it can be found under "services" or "account information." The account holder has the option to choose which month's financial statement they need to view. The statement can then be downloaded to the local device in a PDF format.

The bank statements are the same whether the person receives a paper or electronic copy. Which choice you receive is a question of personal interest, as long as the bank offers both.

People may opt to get their bank statement online for reasons such as:

- **Sustainability.** The length of a bank statement might range from a few pages to several hundred. By opting for an online bank statement, both paper and time can be saved. Furthermore, banks usually keep statements online for several years, making them available at any time.
- **Privacy.** Online bank statements are often more secure than traditionally posted bank statements. The personal information of a person may not be secure through posted bank statements. To secure accounts and personal information, most banks employ a variety of online security methods.

Is the Bank Required to Send You a Monthly Statement on Your Checking or Savings Account?

Yes, in many cases. If electronic fund transfers (EFTs) can be made to or from your account, banks must provide statements at least monthly summarizing any EFTs that occurred each month. The statements include information about each transaction, including transaction-related fees, and beginning and ending account balances. The bank must provide quarterly statements even if no EFTs occurred.

In any case, if the bank provides periodic statements, at least quarterly the statements must include:

- The annual percentage yield (APY) earned during the statement period, using that term.

- The dollar amount of interest earned during the statement period, and whether it was credited.
- The type and dollar amount of any fees that were debited from the account during the statement period.
- The total number of days in the statement period, or the beginning and ending dates of the period.

(Source: "Is the Bank Required to Send Me a Monthly Statement on My Checking or Savings Account?" Office of the Comptroller of the Currency (OCC).)

Correcting Mistakes on Your Bank Statement

Though errors and mistakes in bank statements may occur very rarely, noticing a mistake on the bank statement may be stressful, especially if the account holder reconciles their account often. If you happen to find an error, the concerned bank must be contacted as soon as possible to rectify the situation.

To fix any inaccuracies on a bank statement, the following procedures have to be followed:

- **Verifying the mistake.** If you find a mistake, take the time to double-check that it is indeed a mistake. If at all possible, put across any proof of the error.
- **Contacting the bank.** Make a call to your bank and let them know about the error. You may do this by phoning the bank's customer care department, sending a secure message through your online bank account, or sending an e-mail, depending on the financial institution. If you are calling your bank, let them know you have proof of the issue and inquire about the best method to communicate it.
- **Keeping track of the issue.** It is a good idea to maintain track of any contact you have with your bank or a third-party vendor in case there are any problems later. Keep track of the names of the persons you communicate with, as well as the date and time of your conversations.

Frequently Asked Questions regarding Bank Statement

How Long Should a Person Keep a Bank Statement?

A person may need to keep track of their bank statements from earlier years in various situations, such as when applying for a loan. Banks must preserve records of your bank statements for at least five years by law, and you should be able to retrieve them during that time frame – even if your account has been closed. You may be charged a small amount to view statements that are more than a year or two old, depending on the bank.

Is Bank Statement and a Transaction History the Same?

Transaction history is different from a bank statement. Transaction history is a record of all transactions for a specific bank account over a specified time period. A bank statement typically only covers one month's worth of transactions and may not include current or ongoing transactions.

Can Anyone Check Your Bank Statement?

No. Banks do not reveal information about your bank statement to unknown third parties without your consent.

References

1. Barone, Adam. "Bank Statement," Investopedia, April 1, 2021.
2. Marquit, Miranda. "What Is a Bank Statement?" The Balance, April 30, 2021.
3. Payne, Kevin. "Understanding Your Bank Statement," *Forbes*, July 30, 2020.
4. Kumok, Zina. "What Is a Bank Statement and How Do I Read It?" Dollar Sprout, March 1, 2021.

CHAPTER 22

WHAT YOU SHOULD KNOW ABOUT CHECKING ACCOUNTS

About This Chapter: Text beginning with the heading "What Is a Checking Account?" is excerpted from "Opening a Bank Account," Federal Trade Commission (FTC), September 28, 2012; Text under the heading "Managing Your Checking Account" is excerpted from "Managing Your Checking Account," Consumer Financial Protection Bureau (CFPB), February 3, 2016.

What Is a Checking Account?

When people talk about bank accounts, they usually mean checking accounts. A checking account lets you keep your money safe and still be able to spend it.

A checking account lets you pay for things without using cash. Instead, you might pay with a check or a debit card.

Why Would You Open a Checking Account?

You might open a checking account:

- To keep your money safe
- To pay using a debit card or check, instead of cash
- To get cash from an automated teller machine, or ATM
- To pay your bills online using your checking account
- To get access to loans, depending on your credit history
- To cash checks or wire money
- To earn a little extra money. Some banks pay interest on money in checking accounts. That means the money in your account will earn more money.

Many banks and credit unions charge less for these services if you have an account there.

Managing Your Checking Account

To be successful with your checking account, you first need to choose an appropriate product to meet your needs.

The Importance of Good Checking Account Management

Once you have your checking account, you need to manage it in order to keep it. Good account management helps you to avoid unnecessary fees and helps you to maintain the account. If you have trouble keeping enough money in your account to cover your payments or withdrawals, your bank or credit union might close the account and report you to a checking account reporting company. If there is a negative report, you could have trouble opening a new checking account with a financial institution for up to 7 years. Checking account reporting companies must comply with the Fair Credit Reporting Act (FCRA). This means, for example, that they must follow reasonable procedures to maximize the accuracy of the information that they provide to banks, and they cannot include most information that is more than 7 years old. They can choose a shorter time period, and the checking account reporting companies typically disregard information that is more than five years old.

Here are some tips for reducing the fees on your checking or prepaid account:

Pay Attention to Monthly Service Fees

Many financial institutions waive monthly service fees if you maintain a minimum balance or sign up for direct deposit. Some institutions waive these fees for senior citizens, students, or members of the military. Be sure to ask about these products if you think you might be eligible.

Keep Track of Your Balance and Any Outstanding Payments

Keep track of your account balance and your account activity to avoid spending more than you have in your account. Keeping track of your balance also helps you to keep the minimum balance you need in your account to avoid monthly fees. Some of the steps you can take are:

- Monitor your account online or on your phone.
- Check your balance by phone or online before you withdraw cash at an ATM.
- Check your balance by phone or online before you write a big check or make a big payment.
- Sign up for transaction alerts and low-balance warnings via e-mail or text.
- Do not assume that the money you deposited is available immediately. Find out when the money you deposit will be available for your use. Ask if there is a "hold" on the money you deposit, and if so when the hold will be lifted.
- The payments that you make can be processed very quickly, so do not make a payment from your checking account unless the money to cover it is already in your account and past any hold period.
- Know that your payments and withdrawals are not always processed in the order in which you make them. Be sure that you have enough in your account to cover everything.

- Know when regular electronic transfers, such as a rent payment or utility bills, will be paid.

Avoid Overdraft Fees

An overdraft occurs when you spend or withdraw more money than you have in your account and the bank or credit union pays to cover the shortfall. Overdrafts can be very expensive. Fees are generally charged "per item" and often as high as $35 or more per each overdraft transaction. To resolve an overdraft, you generally have to pay back the amount of the negative balance plus all fees, and you may have to pay additional fees if you do not repay quickly.

To reduce the likelihood that you will overdraft, you can:

- Switch to a checking account that is designed not to allow overdraft. Such "no-overdraft" products can help you manage your spending, but can still charge you a fee if you overspend. For example, if you write a check or try to pay a bill when you do not have enough money in your account, even if the transaction is declined.
- Choose not to "opt-in" to debit overdraft. Your bank or credit union cannot charge you a fee for an overdraft with your debit card unless you "opt-in" to overdraft coverage for these transactions. Keep in mind that you could be charged a fee for checks and online or direct debit ("ACH") overdrafts even if you have chosen not to opt-in.
- Link your accounts. If you link your account, if you run out of money in your checking account, the bank will pull money from the place you have chosen. You can link your checking account to a savings account, if you have one and are able to maintain a balance in it to cover potential shortfalls. You pay a fee for this service, but the fee is usually much lower than an overdraft fee. You may also be able to link your checking account to a credit card or line of credit, if you have one. While the fee you are charged on your checking account may be much lower than an overdraft fee, you may also be charged a fee on the credit card or line of credit.

> **Tip:** Do not let terminology confuse you. "No overdraft" products are designed to help you manage your spending and reduce the likelihood that you will overdraft. Banks and credit unions also offer overdraft programs, such as "overdraft coverage" and "overdraft protection," that generally do allow overdrafts.

Open and Review All of the Statements from Your Bank or Credit Union

Whether you get your account statements by mail, online, or both, review account statements every month to make sure they are correct and report errors immediately. Also watch for changes in your minimum balance requirement, fees, or other account terms.

Spend Only What You Have

Never write a check or authorize an electronic payment for funds unless you know you will have enough money in your account to cover it. If you do not have the funds you will be charged a nonsufficient funds (NSFs) fee or an overdraft fee (for debit card payments and ATM withdrawals, only if you have opted in to overdraft) from the bank or credit union. Overdrawing your account or not paying fees could severely impact your ability to access financial services in the future.

Use Your Financial Institution's ATMs

When you use ATMs in your bank's or credit union's network, there is generally no charge. However, many banks and credit unions will charge you for using an out-of-network ATM, such as an ATM branded by another bank or credit union. The owner of the out-of-network ATM may also charge you a fee. Some banks and credit unions will reimburse you for fees you pay at ATMs on other networks. Many banks and credit unions offer ATM locator maps on their websites and mobile apps to help you find in-network ATMs.

CHAPTER 23
HOW TO BALANCE A CHECKING ACCOUNT

Learning to balance a checking account or a checkbook is crucial for budgeting purposes. It is also termed "reconciling your account" and helps you keep track of your funds (monthly income and expenditures). The account holder checks to see if their expenditure and income records tally with the bank's statement. Balancing a checkbook or a checking account helps the customer plan for future purchases, avoid penalties due to overdrafts, track any fraudulent transactions, and stay updated on interest earnings. Balancing checking accounts has several advantages such as:

- Helping to track purchases, especially if funds are limited
- Helping to recognize any erroneous transactions
- Keeping track of monthly payments such as insurance, utilities, and others
- Preventing overdrawing from the account by maintaining a provision for small amounts such as fees in the monthly budgets

One can track their checking accounts manually using a spreadsheet, a checkbook ledger, or an app. With the correct information at hand, balancing a checking account or the checkbook is quite simple with a few basic steps, including:

- **Writing and matching transactions.** Cross-check every purchase and income with the same in the provided statement and write them down in the checkbook register. One can choose to do this immediately or at the end of the month.
- **Going through the listed numbers.** Use a calculator and go through the transactions to avoid mistakes in amounts. Calculate the numbers twice or thrice to ensure that they match. A simple way to do this is to start calculating with "0," add the total bank balance, add the total deposits, and subtract the total withdrawals. You will end up with the listed amount on the checkbook.

- **Updating the account's balance.** Once the transactions are listed, if there are any discrepancies and if the missing information is available in the bank statement or the record of bills, make sure to update the checkbook register with the new information to avoid confusion.
- **Repeating the process.** It is safer to balance the account often to help catch any unauthorized deductions or incomes. It also helps to stay within the budget allocated and avoid unnecessary expenditure. The account is balanced if the personal account of transactions matches with the bank statement and if the total amount calculated tallies with the starting balance of the bank statement.
- **Fixing errors.** If there is even a slight mismatch between the calculated amount and that reflected in the statement, try to find the mistake as soon as possible. If you need assistance, contact the bank immediately to help figure out the error.

A simple tip to remember is that when balancing a checking account, the total sum of credits and debits (deposits and withdrawals) and the statement's starting balance must be equal to the current balance in the account.

Maintaining the checking account is as essential as balancing it. Some maintenance tips include:

- **Setting a balance.** Every month, make sure to keep a sizable balance remaining in the account for emergencies. Try not to take from this amount for any expenses. This habit may help avoid incurring penalties for insufficient funds.
- **Overdraft protection.** The bank can provide a line of credit at a fee of around $25 to avoid bounced payments that may incur a penalty. This assistance is called "overdraft protection."
- **Go online.** Enlist for online banking services that the bank may provide to help you stay updated with the account.
- **Use ATMs.** ATMs provide easy and secure access to account details such as providing a quick statement, quick cash, displaying the remaining balance, and summaries of deductions.
- **Utilize the potential of electronic notifications.** Signing up for e-mails and texts from the bank can help you track your account on the go. Alerts about frauds, unauthorized large purchases, deposits, account balance details, and low balances can be helpful.

References

1. Pritchard, Justin. "How to Balance a Checking Account," The Balance, May 31, 2021.

2. Caldwell, Miriam. "7 Reasons to Balance Your Bank Accounts Each Month," The Balance, April 30, 2021.
3. Folger, Jean. "The Complete Guide to Checking Accounts," Investopedia, December 11, 2020.
4. Porter, TJ. "Three Reasons You Should Balance Your Checking Account," Bankrate, November 5, 2020.
5. Hood, Eddy. "Bookkeeping: Balancing and Maintaining a Checking Account," Ignite Spot Accounting, March 25, 2020.
6. "How to Balance Your Checking Account," Ramsey Solutions, March 10, 2021.

CHAPTER 24
CREDIT UNION

About This Chapter: This chapter includes text excerpted from "Find, Join or Start a Credit Union," MyCreditUnion.gov, December 1, 2020.

What Is a Credit Union?

Credit unions are not-for-profit organizations that exist to serve their members. Like banks, credit unions accept deposits, make loans and provide a wide array of other financial services. But, as member-owned and cooperative institutions, credit unions provide a safe place to save and borrow at reasonable rates.

You Are More than a Member, You Are Part Owner

Credit unions are owned and controlled by the people, or members, who use their services. Your vote counts. A volunteer board of directors is elected by members to manage a credit union. Credit unions operate to promote the well-being of their members.

Profits made by credit unions are returned back to members in the form of reduced fees, higher savings rates and lower loan rates. Members of a credit union share a common bond, also known as the "credit union's field of membership." Use the information below to find, join or even start a credit union.

Find a Credit Union

Use NCUA's Credit Union Locator (www.mycreditunion.gov/about-credit-unions/credit-union-locator) to locate a credit union near you. Search for a credit union by address, credit union name or charter number. Select a credit union from your search results and view basic information.

Note: Credit union data is refreshed within two business days.

Join a Credit Union

Selecting a Credit Union to Join

After you find a credit union, review the credit union's field of membership to see if you can join. Often, you can find a field of membership information on the credit union's website. Look for wording on membership eligibility, how to join or how to become a member.

How Do You Choose a Credit Union to Join?

Anyone can join a credit union, as long as you are within the credit union's field of membership. This is the common bond between members.

The common bond could be your:

- **Employer.** Many employers sponsor their own credit unions.
- **Family.** Most credit unions allow members' families to join.
- **Geographic Location.** Many credit unions serve anyone that lives, works, worships or attends school in a particular geographic area.
- **Membership in a group** such as a place of worship, school, labor union or homeowners' association may qualify you to join.

What Do You Need to Join a Credit Union?

About $5 to $25, which is generally the cost of purchasing one par value share at a credit union in order to establish a membership account. Some credit unions may also charge a nominal fee to process the account opening.

Start a Credit Union

Are you thinking about starting a federal credit union that would help you and others where you work, or who are members of an association or your community?

Chartering application guidance: Please contact the NCUA's Office of Credit Union Resources and Expansion at 703-518-1150 or NewFCU@ncua.gov for guidance on starting a new federal credit union. A CURE staff member can discuss in greater detail with you the step-by-step processes and answer your questions concerning your specific proposed federal credit union.

Credit Union Field of Membership

A credit union field of membership is a common bond amongst its members. The field of membership of a credit union is a part of its official charter, and is the legal definition of who is eligible to join the credit union. The common bond could be your employer, family, geographic location or membership in a group.

Federally versus Privately Insured Credit Unions

Federally chartered credit unions are regulated by NCUA and insured by the National Credit Union Share Insurance Fund, which is backed by the full faith and credit of the United States government. Established by Congress in 1970 to insure member share accounts at federally insured credit unions, the NCUSIF is similar to the FDIC's deposit insurance coverage.

It is important to note that some deposits at state-chartered credit unions are insured by private insurers. These private insurers provide nonfederal share insurance coverage of deposits that are not backed by the full faith and credit of the United States government.

How Do You Know If Your Credit Union Is Federally Insured?

All federally insured credit unions must prominently display the official NCUA insurance sign at each teller station and where insured account deposits are normally received in their principal place of business and in all branches. Federally insured credit unions are also required to display the official sign on their Internet page, if any, where they accept deposits or open accounts.

All federal credit unions must be insured by NCUA, and no credit union may terminate its federal insurance without first notifying its members.

CHAPTER 25
ELECTRONIC FUND TRANSFER

About This Chapter: Text under the heading "Online Banking" is excerpted from "Online and Mobile Banking Tips for Beginners," Consumer Financial Protection Bureau (CFPB), May 5, 2020; Text under the heading "Online Payment Services," is © 2017 Omnigraphics.

Online Banking

As long as you have a computer or smartphone with access to the Internet and an account with a bank or credit union account eligible for Internet banking, it is easy to get started.

1. **Gather your account numbers**
   Your account numbers should be on your paper statement. Your account number will also be on the bottom of your checks or deposit slips. They are needed to enroll your account.
2. **Find your bank or credit union's website**
   Look on one of your paper statements or on the back of your debit or credit card to find the website, rather than googling or clicking on links in an e-mail or text. If you visit your bank's website from your smartphone, you may be prompted to download the bank or credit union's mobile app that you can use from your phone.
3. **Register for access to your bank or credit union's online banking platform**
   The first time you visit, you will follow the prompts to create an online account. You will answer questions to prove it is really you, choose a username and password, and set up security features and preferences. Be sure to create strong passwords and do not use the same password for all accounts. Do not use information such as addresses and birthdays in your passwords.
4. **Log in and take a tutorial**
   If it is offered by your bank or credit union to learn your way around the platform.

What Can You Do with Online and Mobile App Banking?

- Most transactions can be done online or through your financial institution's mobile app on your smartphone.
- Check your account balances online at any time. You now can catch errors such as unauthorized activity earlier – without having to wait for your paper statement. You usually can notify your bank or credit union account of errors through the online or mobile banking app or chat functions.
- Often, you can see deposits and charges that are pending, meaning they have not posted to your account yet. Note that for pending debit card transactions, the amounts you see may not be the same as the final amount that posts to your account. Be sure to check your bank's or credit union's funds availability policy before assuming that pending deposits are available for making payments or withdrawals.
- Consider whether you would like to continue to receive paper versions of your periodic statements and other documents. Your bank or credit union may prompt you to go paperless while you set up online banking.
- Most banks and credit unions allow you to set up automatic notifications to help you manage your account and alert you when any of the following happen: A direct deposit is received, a large payment is charged, your balance falls below a certain amount, your account is in overdraft, and more. Often, bank and credit union online portals offer you the ability to sign up to get these alerts via text, e-mail, or both. These alerts can help ensure you stay informed without having to log in to your account several times a day.
- Most banks and credit unions will allow you to deposit checks using your smartphone and a mobile app. You might not be able to deposit all types of checks this way, so check with your bank or credit union if you have any questions. The mobile app makes it easy to deposit a check in a few steps:
  - Download your bank or credit union's app on your smartphone if you have not already.
  - Understand any rules your bank or credit union has about mobile check deposit.
  - Follow the directions in the mobile app to deposit the check.
  - Hold onto the check for several days after deposit until you are sure it has posted to your account meaning that it is no longer pending and any holds your institution has placed have expired.
  - Destroy the check once it is cleared by shredding it or tearing or cutting it up.
- If you need to transfer money between accounts, or even between financial institutions, your online banking or mobile app likely offers you options to do that. Make sure you understand the terms and conditions of your transfer

and double check that you are using the correct account and routing numbers when making any transfers.

- There is a good chance your financial institution offers a way to send money person to person, too. Before you use any mobile payment services, check out our best practices guide to make sure your transactions are done safely. You can test it out by transferring a small amount, like a dollar, back and forth. That way you will be sure your money goes where you want and you receive money you are owed.
- Instead of writing checks and mailing them, you can pay most bills online or through the mobile app for your financial institution.
- Banking online or through your mobile device is secure, as long as you follow best practices for keeping the information on your mobile device safe. Your financial institution may offer additional services to help you keep your account safe, including turning off your debit card if you suspect fraud. Check with your bank or credit union to learn more about additional protections they may offer.

How Do You Get Help with Online Banking?

If you run into any issues, ask for help! If you need specific guidance, contact your bank or credit union directly. Customer service associates are available by phone, online chat, or video in some cases. The financial institution staff will help you set up your account and answer questions. They will also help you figure out what you can and cannot do online or through their app. Please note that during this pandemic crisis, many bank and credit union call centers are experiencing high call volumes and may be delayed in responding to inquiries.

Online Payment Services

An increasing numbers are using online payment services, such as PayPal, Venmo, Zelle®, etc., to process their transactions and the advantages are clear. From the seller perspective, merchants do not need to set up complicated technology and financial infrastructure to take funds via the web. Instead they pay a fee to the service, which handles the transaction. And buyers enjoy advantages such as convenience, payment flexibility and a higher level of information security.

Using Online Payment Services

Online payments can be made in a variety of ways, including with credit cards, debit cards, gift cards, eChecks, and mobile phone apps. But more and more, online payment services are becoming a method of choice, both for individual sellers and for the websites of large companies. Although services vary somewhat, here is how the process generally works:

- Go to the payment service's website and sign up for a free account.

- Link the account to your credit card, debit card, or bank account.
- Send money to anyone with an e-mail address.
- Receive money from anyone who has an account with that service.

When you send money, it is charged to your credit card or deducted from your bank account. When you receive money, it can be deposited directly into your account or you can request a check in the mail. Some services also have their own debit cards that allow you to get cash from an ATM or make purchases.

Advantages and Disadvantages of Online Payment Services

Online payment services have become so popular because they offer a number of advantages over other forms of making purchases on the web. Some of these include:

- **Convenience.** Online retailers and auction sites that take payments from services generally link to those services making it easy for you to transfer funds.
- **Security.** Rather than having your credit card number or other financial information held by every online store and individual you do business with, that data can be maintained by just one service.
- **Flexibility.** Most online payment services allow you to shop with online merchants, buy from individual sellers, have money sent to you at college, and send funds to someone who needs it.
- **Easy access to funds.** When you sell something or get money from an individual, you can generally use your payment service account to buy goods and services online, have money sent to you as a check or bank transfer, or, in some cases, get a debit card that can be used anywhere.

Of course, there are some disadvantages, as well, such as:

- **There can be fees.** Most online payment services allow buyers to create an account and conduct certain transactions at no cost, but some have limits on the amount of business that can be transacted for free, after which fees are added. And all of them charge sellers a fee that is usually based on the amount sold.
- **Lack of regulation.** Online payment services function in many ways such as a bank, taking in money, holding it, and paying it out when requested. Yet they are not subject to the same regulations as banks. For example, money held by a payment service is not insured by the Federal Deposit Insurance Corporation (FDIC) as it would be when deposited in a bank.
- **Fraud.** Since many transactions handled by payment services are between individual buyers and sellers, rather than through company websites, there is always the possibility that you could find yourself doing business with an unscrupulous person. If you buy something and do not get it if it is not

what you thought you were buying, or if you sell something and do not get your payment, there will be a process for resolving the issue, but it could take some time.

- **Hacking.** While it is true that online payment services offer the security of having your card or bank account information stored in just one place, there is always the chance that the service's system could be invaded by a hacker stealing customer data. In such a case, it is likely that account holders will eventually be compensated, but the process could be complex and take a long time.
- **Slow customer service.** With many payment services, if something goes wrong with a transaction, it can be difficult to speak to a customer service representative. Most of the services are set up to take complaints online, with automated responses. There is almost always a way to resolve problems, but it can be time-consuming and frustrating.

Some Common Online Payment Services

There are quite a few online payment services available to buyers and sellers. Some are aimed at facilitating individual transactions, like auctions, while others are designed for use by merchants with their own dedicated websites. A few of these services include:

- Amazon Payments
- Dwolla
- PayPal
- Skrill
- 2Checkout
- Venmo
- Zelle®

Online Payment Security

Payment security issues are not the exclusive domain of online transactions, of course – they can also be a problem at physical stores – but online payments cause extra concern on the part of consumers, so it pays to be familiar with some of the steps you can take to protect yourself:

- Do some research before committing to an online payment service. Go to their websites and see what kind of security measures they use. Also, do a web search for reviews of the service to see what other consumers have to say about them.
- Use strong passwords. Even if online payment websites do not require complex passwords, you can create your own by using a combination of numbers, symbols, and a mix of capital and lowercase letters.
- Use different passwords for each online account or payment service. Once a hacker figures out one of your passwords, you do not want the criminal to

have access to all your online accounts. At least use different passwords for online purchases and other financial transactions than you do for e-mail and social media.

- Install antivirus and antimalware software and a firewall on your computer. This is all-around good practice, but it is especially important if you do any financial transactions online, including sending funds through a payment service.

EFT Stop Payment Privileges

When you use an electronic fund transfer, the EFT Act does not give you the right to stop payment. If your purchase is defective or your order is not delivered, it is as if you paid cash: it is up to you to resolve the problem with the seller and get your money back. There is one exception. If you arranged for recurring payments out of your account to third parties, such as insurance companies or utilities, you can stop payment if you notify your institution at least three business days before the scheduled transfer. You can notify the bank orally or in writing.

(Source: "Electronic Fund Transfers," MyCreditUnion.gov.)

References

1. Hord, Jennifer. "How Electronic Payment Works," HowStuffWorks.com, October 19, 2005.
2. McIver, Rich. "Online Payment Processing 101," CleverBridge.com, November 4, 2015.
3. O'Brien, Russell. "Online Payment Basics," HubPages.com, December 15, 2016.
4. Smith, Aaron; Anderson, Monica. "Online Shopping and E-commerce," Pew Research Center, December 19, 2016.
5. Whitehouse, Jordan. "Types of eCommerce Payment Systems," Techwalla.com, March 31, 2015.

CHAPTER 26

MOBILE PAYMENTS AND MOBILE WALLETS

About This Chapter: Text beginning with the heading "What Is a Mobile Payment?" is excerpted from "Mobile Payments and Mobile Wallets," MyCreditUnion.gov, November 28, 2018; Text under the heading "Mobile Wallet Services Protection" is excerpted from "Mobile Wallet Services Protection," Federal Communications Commission (FCC), February 25, 2020.

What Is a Mobile Payment?

A mobile payment uses your mobile phone or other mobile device, online or in person, to provide information electronically to make a payment. There are many different technologies and processes used to make mobile payments and new ones are always around the corner.

Common Types of Mobile Payments

Near field communication (NFC) mobile wallet payment. NFC enables you to tap or wave your mobile device close to a "reader" next to a cash register or on a vending machine, turnstile, parking meter, etc. Your mobile device sends the account information that you are going to use for the payment through a radio signal with a short range of about four inches. The mobile wallet app stores your account number in a secure chip in the phone or in a secure file server linked to the mobile wallet app. Examples include Apple Pay and Google Android Pay.

Mobile web payments (WAP). Use the web browser on your mobile device or a mobile app to make a purchase on the Internet and charge it to your credit, debit, prepaid or bank account.

QR code (quick response) scans. Your mobile device produces a QR code on the screen to be scanned at the register. The QR code provides the link to the payment information. Usually, you download a mobile app for the merchant (such as Starbucks) or a mobile wallet (such as LevelUp) that allows you to create the QR code on your mobile device.

Mobile text payments (SMS). Send a code by text message to the seller using your mobile device to approve the payment. The purchase is charged to your wireless service bill or a prepaid account held by the mobile operator. Personal information, such as payment account number, should not be sent via SMS.

Direct mobile billing. Provide your mobile phone number as your account number to the merchant. The purchase is charged to your wireless service bill. These are normally low-dollar digital payments for items such as ringtones, screensavers, or apps, with most mobile operators establishing a transaction and consolidated dollar limit.

Types of Internet Frauds

- Phishing or spoofing involves the usage of fake e-mails, text messages, or copycat websites to commit identity theft. Or, it can be used to steal personal information including credit card and bank account numbers, debit card PINs, and account passwords.
- Data breaches occur when sensitive data (personal or financial information) is hacked into, leaked, or inadvertently posted from a secure location. This information may be used to steal identities or commit financial fraud.
- Malware is dangerous software that is designed to disable computers and computer systems.
- Internet auction fraud involves the misrepresentation of products from an Internet auction site. Or, it can occur when merchandise is not delivered to a buyer by a seller online as promised.
- Credit card fraud occurs when scammers fraudulently acquire credit or debit card numbers to obtain money or property.

(Source: "Online Safety," USA.gov.)

Protecting Your Privacy and Security When You Make Mobile Payments

Did you know that now you can use a smartphone, tablet or other mobile devices to pay for some purchases? Mobile payments can be convenient – no need to write a check or to pull out your wallet for cash or plastic. No need to type in your payment information to buy something online. But, are mobile payments safe? What about your privacy? Those are good questions to ask when you consider using any new technology. Because you usually carry your phone or other mobile device with you, it is on most of the time, and it may contain very sensitive personal information, it is especially important to keep it, and its contents, safe and secure, especially if you want to use it to make mobile payments or conduct other financial business.

What Is a Mobile Wallet?

A mobile wallet stores payment card information on your mobile device or smartwatch and allows you to make electronic purchases.

Mobile wallet security. Purchases made using a mobile wallet may be more secure than physical cards. This is because mobile wallets use methods such as data encryption and tokenization to monitor and secure your personal and payment card account information.

Mobile Wallet Services Protection

Many consumers use their smartphones, tablets and other mobile devices as mobile wallets to pay for goods and services, using apps to make both online and in-person purchases. As our use of mobile payment services increases, so does the need to protect mobile devices, apps and associated data from theft and cyber attacks.

How to Safeguard Your Mobile Wallet

- Never leave your smartphone unattended in a public place or visible in an unattended car.
- Consider your surroundings and use your smartphone or mobile device discreetly.
- Never use mobile payment services over an unsecured Wi-Fi network. (See our consumer guide: www.fcc.gov/wireless-security.)
- Choose unique passwords for all your mobile apps.
- Install and maintain security software on your smartphone. Apps are available to:
    - Locate your smartphone from any computer.
    - Lock your smartphone to restrict access.
    - Wipe sensitive personal information and mobile wallet credentials from your smartphone.
    - Make your smartphone emit a loud sound ("scream") to help you or the police locate it.
- Be careful about using social networking apps, which may pose a security risk and may possibly allow unwanted access to personal information, including your mobile financial data.
- Monitor financial accounts linked to in mobile apps for any fraudulent charges. Review the service agreements for these accounts to find out what steps to take if your smartphone is lost, stolen or hacked, and what charges you may be responsible for paying.
- The police may need your smartphone's unique identifying information if it is stolen or lost. Write down the make, model number, serial number and unique device identification number – either the International Mobile Equipment Identifier (IMEI) or the Mobile Equipment Identifier (MEID) number. Some phones display the IMEI/MEID number when you dial *#06#. The IMEI/MEID also can be found on a label located beneath the phone's battery or on the box that came with the phone.

What to Do If Your Mobile Device Is Lost or Stole

- If you are not certain whether your smartphone or mobile device has been stolen, or if you have simply misplaced it, try locating the smartphone by calling it or by using the security software's GPS locator.

- If you have installed security software on your smartphone, use it to lock the device, wipe sensitive personal information and/or activate the alarm.
- Immediately report the theft or loss to your wireless carrier. If you provide your carrier with the IMEI or MEID number, your carrier may be able to disable your smartphone and mobile payment apps, and block access to your personal information and sensitive data. Request written confirmation from your carrier that you reported the smartphone as missing and that the smartphone was disabled.
- Report the theft to the police – including the make and model, serial and IMEI or MEID number in your report. Some service providers require proof that the smartphone was stolen and a police report can provide that documentation.
- If you are unable to lock your stolen or lost smartphone, change all of your passwords for mobile payment apps and any bank or credit card accounts that you have accessed using your smartphone service, then contact those financial institutions about the loss or theft.

PART 4 | CREDIT CARDS AND CREDIT SCORES

CHAPTER 27

CREDIT HISTORY

About This Chapter: This chapter includes text excerpted from "Your Credit History," Federal Trade Commission (FTC), September 28, 2012.

What Is a Credit History?

Sometimes, people talk about your credit. What they mean is your credit history. Your credit history describes how you use money:

- How many credit cards do you have?
- How many loans do you have?
- Do you pay your bills on time?

If you have a credit card or a loan from a bank, you have a credit history. Companies collect information about your loans and credit cards.

Companies also collect information about how you pay your bills. They put this information in one place: your credit report.

People sometimes confuse the words debt and credit because they are both connected to borrowing money. Credit is your ability to borrow money if you want a loan or mortgage. Debt is the money you owe when you take on a loan.

(Source: "Your Money, Your Goals – a Financial Empowerment Toolkit for Community Volunteers," Consumer Financial Protection Bureau (CFPB).)

What Is a Credit Report?

Your credit report is a summary of your credit history. It lists:

- Your name, address, and Social Security number
- Your credit cards
- Your loans
- How much money you owe
- If you pay your bills on time or late

Why Do You Have a Credit Report?

Businesses want to know about you before they lend you money. Would you want to lend money to someone who pays bills on time? Or to someone who always pays late?

Businesses look at your credit report to learn about you. They decide if they want to lend you money, or give you a credit card. Sometimes, employers look at your credit report when you apply for a job. Cell phone companies and insurance companies look at your credit report, too.

Who Makes Your Credit Report?

A company called a "credit reporting company" collects your information. There are three big credit reporting companies:

- TransUnion
- Equifax
- Experian

These companies write and keep a report about you.

Can You See Your Credit Report?

You can get a free copy of your credit report every year. That means one copy from each of the three companies that writes your reports.

The law says you can get your free credit reports if you:

- Call Annual Credit Report at 877-322-8228 or
- Go to AnnualCreditReport.com

Someone might say you can get a free report at another website. They probably are not telling the truth.

What Is a Credit Score?

A credit score is a number. It is based on your credit history. But, it does not come with your free credit report unless you pay for it.

A high credit score means you have good credit. A low credit score means you have bad credit. Different companies have different scores. Low scores are around 300. High scores are around 700–850.

Do You Need to Get Your Credit Score?

It is very important to know what is in your credit report. But, a credit score is a number that matches your credit history. If you know your history is good, your score will be good. You can get your credit report for free.

It costs money to find out your credit score. Sometimes a company might say the score is free. But, if you look closely, you might find that you signed up for a service that checks your credit for you. Those services charge you every month.

Before you pay any money, ask yourself if you need to see your credit score. It might be interesting. But, is it worth paying money for?

What If You Do Not Have Credit?

You might not have a credit history if:

- You have not had credit card
- You have not gotten a loan from a bank or credit union

Without a credit history, it can be harder to get a job, an apartment, or even a credit card. It sounds crazy: You need credit to get credit.

How Do You Get Credit?

Do you want to build your credit history? You will need to pay bills that are included in a credit report.

- Sometimes, utility companies put information into a credit report. Do you have utility bills in your name? That can help build credit.
- Many credit cards put information into credit reports.
- Sometimes, you can get a store credit card that can help build credit.
- A secured credit card also can help you build your credit.

Why Is Your Credit Report Important?

Businesses look at your credit report when you apply for:

- Loans from a bank
- Credit cards
- Jobs
- Insurance

If you apply for one of these, the business wants to know if you pay your bills. The business also wants to know if you owe money to someone else. The business uses the information in your credit report to decide whether to give you a loan, a credit card, a job, or insurance.

What Does "Good Credit" Mean?

Some people have good credit. Some people have bad credit. Some people do not have a credit history. Businesses see this in your credit report. Different things happen based on your credit history:

You Have a "Good" credit

That means:

- You have more loan choices
- It is easier to get credit cards

- You pay lower interest rates
- You pay less for loans and credit cards

You Have a "Bad" credit

That means:

- You have fewer loan choices
- It is harder to get credit cards
- You pay higher interest rates
- You pay more for loans and credit cards

You Have a "No" credit

That means:

- You have no bank loan choices
- It is very hard to get credit cards
- You pay high-interest rates
- Loans and credit cards are hard to get and cost a lot

All this information is in your credit report.

Why Should You Get Your Credit Report?

An important reason to get your credit report is to find problems or mistakes and fix them:

- You might find somebody's information in your report by mistake.
- You might find information about you from a long time ago.
- You might find accounts that are not yours. That might mean someone stole your identity.

You want to know what is in your report. The information in your report will help decide whether you get a loan, a credit card, a job or insurance.

If the information is wrong, you can try to fix it. If the information is right – but not so good – you can try to improve your credit history.

Where Do You Get Your Free Credit Report?

You can get your free credit report from Annual Credit Report. That is the only free place to get your report. You can get it online: AnnualCreditReport.com, or by phone: 877-322-8228.

You get one free report from each credit reporting company every year. That means you get three reports each year.

What Should You Do When You Get Your Credit Report?

Your credit report has a lot of information. Check to see if the information is correct. Is it your name and address? Do you recognize the accounts listed?

If there is wrong information in your report, try to fix it. You can write to the credit reporting company. Ask them to change the information that is wrong. You might need to send proof that the information is wrong – for example, a copy of a bill that shows the correct information. The credit reporting company must check it out and write back to you.

How Do You Improve Your Credit?

Look at your free credit report. The report will tell you how to improve your credit history. Only you can improve your credit. No one else can fix information in your credit report that is not good, but is correct.

It takes time to improve your credit history. Here are some ways to help rebuild your credit.

- Pay your bills by the date they are due. This is the most important thing you can do.
- Lower the amount you owe, especially on your credit cards. Owing a lot of money hurts your credit history.
- Do not get new credit cards if you do not need them. A lot of new credit hurts your credit history.
- Do not close older credit cards. Having credit for a longer time helps your rating.

After six to nine months of this, check your credit report again. You can use one of your free reports from the Annual Credit Report.

How Does a Credit Score Work?

Your credit score is a number related to your credit history. If your credit score is high, your credit is good. If your credit score is low, your credit is bad.

There are different credit scores. Each credit reporting company creates a credit score. Other companies create scores, too. The range is different, but it usually goes from about 300 (low) to 850 (high).

It costs money to look at your credit score. Sometimes a company might say the score is free. But usually, there is a cost.

What Goes into a Credit Score?

Each company has its own way to calculate your credit score. They look at:

- How many loans and credit cards you have
- How much money you owe
- How long you have had credit
- How much new credit you have

They look at the information in your credit report and give it a number. That is your credit score.

It is very important to know what is in your credit report. If your report is good, your score will be good. You can decide if it is worth paying money to see what number someone gives your credit history.

How Do You Check Your Credit Report?

This is easy to do by phone:

- Call Annual Credit Report at 877-322-8228.
- Answer questions from a recorded system. You have to give your address, Social Security number, and birth date.
- Choose to only show the last four numbers of your Social Security number. It is safer than showing your full Social Security number on your report.
- Choose which credit reporting company you want a report from. (You get one free report from each company every year.)

That company mails your report to you. It should arrive 2–3 weeks after you call.

What Do You Do with a Credit Report?

Read it carefully. Make sure the information is correct:

- **Personal information.** Are the name and address correct?
- **Accounts.** Do you recognize them?
- Is the information correct?
- **Negative information.** Do you recognize the accounts in this section of the report?
- Is the information correct?
- **Inquiries.** Do you recognize the places you applied for credit?

(If you do not, maybe someone stole your identity.)

The report will tell you how to improve your credit history. Only you can improve your credit history. It will take time. But, if any of the information in your report is wrong, you can ask to have it fixed.

How Do You Fix Mistakes in Your Credit Report?

- Write a letter. Tell the credit reporting company that you have questions about information in your report.
- Explain which information is wrong and why you think so.
- Say that you want the information corrected or removed from your report.
- Send a copy of your credit report with the wrong information circled.
- Send copies of other papers that help you explain your opinion.
- Send this information to Certified Mail. Ask the post office for a return receipt. The receipt is proof that the credit reporting company got your letter.

The credit reporting company must look into your complaint and answer you in writing.

How Do You Use Credit?

When you use credit, it usually means using a credit card. It also might mean that you get a loan. A loan is another way to use credit.

Using credit means you borrow money to buy something.

- You borrow money (with your credit card or loan).
- You buy the thing you want.
- You pay back that loan later – with interest.

What Is Interest?

Interest is what you pay for using someone else's money. You repay money to whoever gave you the credit card or loan.

Credit cards and loans have different interest rates. Look for the "APR." APR means annual percentage rate. It is how much interest you pay during a whole year.

A lower interest rate means you pay less money. A higher interest rate means you pay more money.

When Can You Use Credit?

Many people use a credit card to buy everyday things. You might use a credit card to pay for:

- Gas
- Groceries
- Services – such as a haircut

Loans usually are for more expensive things. You might get a loan for:

- Furniture
- Education
- A car or home

Where Can You Get a Credit Card?

Banks and credit unions offer credit cards. They usually offer credit cards to people with a good credit history.

Some stores offer credit cards. You can use a store credit card only in that store. Sometimes these cards are easier to get if you do not have a good credit history. Sometimes a store credit card is a good way to build your credit history.

What If You Cannot Get a Credit Card?

Banks and other companies offer secured credit cards. This means you deposit money with the bank. Then you spend that money by using the secured credit card.

A secured credit card works like a debit card. You use your money, not a loan from a bank. A secured credit card can help you build your credit history.

Where Can You Get a Loan?

Banks and credit unions offer loans. They usually offer loans to people with a good credit history.

Some stores offer loans to buy their product. These loans often cost more money. Why? Because interest often is higher on a store loan than on a bank loan.

What If You Cannot Get a Loan?

There are other ways to borrow money. Some people go to a payday lender. Some use the title to their car to get a loan. Some people pawn things.

These other ways to borrow are expensive. They almost always cost more than going to a bank, a credit union, or a store. Some people have problems with debt after using these ways to borrow. The charges can be very high. It is hard to pay the money back and get out of debt.

CHAPTER 28
USING CREDIT WISELY

The responsible use of credit can have a major impact on a student's future. Obviously, you need to have an established, healthy credit history if you plan to buy a car or home and make other large purchases, but the way you handle credit can also have other significant implications. For example, landlords review credit history before they will rent you an apartment, and many employers check your credit record as part of the hiring process. The smart thing to do is to begin building a positive credit history now, taking small steps to demonstrate your ability to handle money effectively. A good record of repayment will not only make it easier to get the credit you need in the future but will also result in lower interest rates when you do borrow money.

Credit Score

When someone checks your credit history, what they are looking at is your credit score. This is a number, generally from 300 to 850, tallied by large credit reporting agencies (CRAs) using information about past purchases and repayment that is obtained from various retailers and other creditors. The three largest CRAs are Equifax, Experian, and TransUnion, and prospective lenders use their scores as predictors of your likelihood to default on future credit.

There can be more than 30 factors that go into calculating a credit score, but these are generally grouped together into five major categories:

- **Credit history.** This is the most important factor and makes up 35 percent of your credit score. Unsurprisingly, lenders want to know that you regularly pay back money you owe.
- **Total indebtedness.** This makes up 30 percent of the score and is important because having a lot of debt can make it hard to pay it all back. The ratio of debt to available credit is also critical. Having a lot of available credit but only using a small amount is good; using up all or most of your available credit hurts your score.

- **Length of credit history.** Accounting for 15 percent of the total score, this includes both how long you have had a credit record and how long individual accounts have been open. A longer history gives potential lenders a better idea of how you handle credit.
- **Type of credit.** This generally makes up 10 percent of the score, although it is more important for individuals with a short credit history. A mix of different kinds of credit shows potential lenders that you can handle various types of indebtedness responsibly.
- **New credit.** This makes up another 10 percent of the total and includes newly-opened accounts as well as "hard inquiries," which go on your record any time you apply for credit, whether you actually borrow money or not. (Soft inquiries, such as when you check your own credit record, have no impact on your score.) Lenders may see too much new credit – or applying for new credit – as an indication that you will be adding more indebtedness in the near future.

Building a Credit Record

Students building a credit history will need to start small and take carefully measured steps to demonstrate fiscal responsibility. One of the first things to do is to check your current credit history, if you have one. There are several online sites that allow you to do this, including Freecreditreport.com, Annualcreditreport.com, and Creditkarma.com, as well as the three major CRAs. Here are some suggestions for next steps:

- **Open savings and checking accounts.** It is always good to have some savings in the bank, and the regular use of a checking account and debit card shows that you can budget and handle money responsibly.
- **Pay your monthly bills.** Regular payment of phone, electric, and cable bills is another indicator of prudent financial management.
- **Pay your student loans.** Most students need loans to help pay for college, and making payments on time shows that you take your responsibilities seriously.
- **Get a student credit card.** One of the best ways to begin building credit is to select a suitable card with a low credit limit, then use it regularly and make payments in full each month. To start with, you may need a joint card with a parent or other person with established credit.

Note that not all of these go directly into a credit score. For example, the use of a debit card would not have an impact on the total. But, each of these steps provides an indication of financial responsibility and helps develop good money-management habits.

Keep in touch with your creditors. If you cannot make a payment on time, for example, ask for an extension. There is usually not a problem doing this (once, anyway), and it might help you avoid a late fee. If payments are due at a bad time of month for you, ask for a revised due date.

Types of Credit

There are a number of kinds of credit that are commonly available to students, and it is important to understand how they work. Unless you have an established credit history, it is likely that you will need a cosigner or joint account holder, but as long as your name is on the account, you will be building a positive credit history.

- **Credit cards.** These are cards, such as Visa, Mastercard, and Discover, issued by a bank or other financial institution that you can use to purchase goods or services. The card-issuer pays the merchant or service provider, then you pay back the money to the issuer. About one-third of college students have a credit card of some kind, because they are a convenient way to pay expenses and buy things on campus. But, if you do not pay off the entire balance each month, a finance charge will be added, and this will continue to build until the balance is paid off. Look for a card with no annual fee and the lowest interest rate possible.
- **Retail cards.** Also called "store cards," these are usually issued by department stores for use at their retail locations or online. They have limited use, since they can only be used with one retailer, and for that reason they are not as common as they once were. (Most retailers now partner with a major credit-card issuer for a store-branded card that can be used anywhere.) But, retail cards have the advantage of generally being easier to get than a major credit card, so they can be a good way to start building credit history.
- **Gasoline cards.** Another type of retail card, these are issued by gasoline companies for use at their own stations. Like store cards, they tend to be easier to get than major credit-card brands, and they are a good way for students with cars to keep track of fuel and maintenance expenses and build a good credit score.
- **Student loans.** Education loans most often come from government-backed sources. Some are based on need and some are open to anyone. Most of the time, repayment is deferred until you graduate or leave school, and interest may also not begin accruing until then. Other student loans come from private sources and work like any other credit instrument, such as a car loan. In either case, maintaining a regular schedule of repayment works to build a strong credit history.

Good Credit Practices

Many people get into trouble by not using credit wisely. Developing solid credit practices while avoiding some common pitfalls can help ensure that you build and maintain a good credit score and create financial health. Here are some tips:

- **Shop for credit.** Fees and interest rates vary widely, and they can really add up. Speak to several lenders and examine their websites carefully before signing anything.
- **Read the fine print.** Credit applications contain a lot of detail. Be sure you know if, for example, you are signing up for a low introductory interest rate that goes up after a period of time.
- **Do not borrow more than you can pay back.** It may seem strange, but lenders will often loan you more money than you can repay. Know your finances and live within your budget.
- **Use cash or a debit card when possible.** Credit cards are convenient, but they let you spend more than you have. Sticking to cash or debit cards limits you to the funds you have on hand.
- **Have only one credit card.** Credit-card offers are tempting, but with multiple cards you run the risk of overextending your debt, and applying for them negatively affects your credit score.
- **Avoid annual fees.** Some credit cards come with an annual fee, but so many of them do not that there is no need to pay for the privilege of having a card.
- **Avoid late fees.** If you do not make payments on time, you will be assessed a late fee. This not only costs money, it also negatively affects your credit score and may result in a higher interest rate.
- **Pay your balance every month.** By paying off the amount you charge each month, you will avoid accruing interest, which costs you money. **Note:** There is a common myth that paying the balance each month has a negative impact on your credit score. This is false. It will help build your score.
- **Do not get cash advances.** Read the fine print. Cash advances on credit cards almost always come with higher interest rates and possibly some additional fees.
- **Take advantage of points and other perks.** When shopping for a credit card, look for one that offers reward points, travel rewards, discounts, and other perks. These can save you money.
- **Check your monthly statements.** You want to be sure the lender's accounting is accurate and that there are no charges you did not initiate. If you find a discrepancy, call the lender immediately.
- **Check your credit score at least annually.** Make sure it is accurate and there are no accounts listed that you did not open. If something looks wrong, contact the lender and the CRA right away.

References

1. "10 Tips for Using Credit Wisely," BusinessWire.com, April 7, 2015.
2. "Credit Basics: Using Credit Wisely," CapitolOne.com, 2017.
3. "How to Use Credit Cards Wisely," CollegeBoard.org, 2017.
4. Irby, LaToya. "Dos and Don'ts of Using Credit Cards Wisely," TheBalance.com, June 26, 2016.
5. "Using Credit Wisely," Greenpath.com, n.d.
6. "Using Credit Wisely," HandsOnBanking.org, n.d.

CHAPTER 29
CREDIT REPAIR

About This Chapter: This chapter includes text excerpted from "Credit Repair: How to Help Yourself," Federal Trade Commission (FTC), November 15, 2012.

You see the ads in newspapers, on TV, and online. You hear them on the radio. You get fliers in the mail, e-mail messages, and maybe even calls offering credit repair services. They all make the same claims:

"Credit problems? No problem!"

"We can remove bankruptcies, judgments, liens, and bad loans from your credit file forever!"

"We can erase your bad credit – 100% guaranteed."

"Create a new credit identity – legally."

Do yourself a favor and save some money, too. Do not believe these claims: they are very likely signs of a scam. Indeed, attorneys at the Federal Trade Commission, the nation's consumer protection agency, say they have never seen a legitimate credit repair operation making those claims. The fact is there is no quick fix for creditworthiness. You can improve your credit report legitimately, but it takes time, a conscious effort, and sticking to a personal debt repayment plan.

Your Rights

No one can legally remove accurate and timely negative information from a credit report. You can ask for an investigation – at no charge to you – of information in your file that you dispute as inaccurate or incomplete. Some people hire a company to investigate for them, but anything a credit repair company can do legally, you can do for yourself at little or no cost. By law:

- You are entitled to a free credit report if a company takes "adverse action" against you, such as denying your application for credit, insurance, or employment. You have to ask for your report within 60 days of receiving notice of the action. The notice includes the name, address, and phone number of the consumer reporting company. You are also entitled to one free report a year if you are unemployed and plan to look for a job within 60 days; if you are on welfare; or if your report is inaccurate because of fraud, including identity theft.

- Each of the nationwide credit reporting companies – Equifax, Experian, and TransUnion – is required to provide you with a free copy of your credit report once every 12 months, if you ask for it. To order, visit annualcreditreport.com, or call 877-322-8228. You may order reports from each of the three credit reporting companies at the same time, or you can stagger your requests throughout the year.
- It does not cost anything to dispute mistakes or outdated items on your credit report. Both the credit reporting company and the information provider (the person, company, or organization that provides information about you to a credit reporting company) are responsible for correcting inaccurate or incomplete information in your report. To take advantage of all your rights, contact both the credit reporting company and the information provider.

Do It Yourself

Step 1: Tell the credit reporting company, in writing, what information you think is inaccurate. Include copies (NOT originals) of any documents that support your position. In addition to including your complete name and address, your letter should identify each item in your report that you dispute; state the facts and the reasons you dispute the information, and ask that it be removed or corrected. You may want to enclose a copy of your report, and circle the items in question. Send your letter by certified mail, "return receipt requested," so you can document that the credit reporting company got it. Keep copies of your dispute letter and enclosures.

Credit reporting companies must investigate the items you question within 30 days – unless they consider your dispute frivolous. They also must forward all the relevant data you provide about the inaccuracy to the organization that provided the information. After the information provider gets notice of a dispute from the credit reporting company, it must investigate, review the relevant information, and report the results back to the credit reporting company. If the investigation reveals that the disputed information is inaccurate, the information provider has to notify the nationwide credit reporting companies so they can correct it in your file.

When the investigation is complete, the credit reporting company must give you the results in writing, too, and a free copy of your report if the dispute results in a change. If an item is changed or deleted, the credit reporting company cannot put the disputed information back in your file unless the information provider verifies that it is accurate and complete. The credit reporting company also must send you written notice that includes the name, address, and phone number of the information provider. If you ask, the credit reporting company must send notices of any correction to anyone who got your report in the past six months. You also can ask that a corrected copy of your report be sent to anyone who got a copy during the past two years for employment purposes.

If an investigation does not resolve your dispute with the credit reporting company, you can ask that a statement of the dispute be included in your file and in future reports. You also can ask the credit reporting company to give your statement to anyone who got a copy of your report in the recent past. You will probably have to pay for this service.

Step 2: Tell the creditor or other information provider, in writing, that you dispute an item. Include copies (NOT originals) of documents that support your position. Many providers specify an address for disputes. If the provider reports the item to a consumer reporting company, it must include a notice of your dispute. And if the information is found to be inaccurate, the provider may not report it again.

Reporting Accurate Negative Information

When negative information in your report is accurate, only time can make it go away. A credit reporting company can report most accurate negative information for seven years and bankruptcy information for 10 years. Information about an unpaid judgment against you can be reported for seven years or until the statute of limitations runs out, whichever is longer. The seven-year reporting period starts from the date the event took place. There is no time limit on reporting information about criminal convictions; information reported in response to your application for a job that pays more than $75,000 a year; and information reported because you have applied for more than $150,000 worth of credit or life insurance.

The Credit Repair Organizations Act

The Credit Repair Organization Act (CROA) makes it illegal for credit repair companies to lie about what they can do for you, and to charge you before they have performed their services. The CROA is enforced by the Federal Trade Commission and requires credit repair companies to explain:

- Your legal rights in a written contract that also details the services they will perform
- Your three day right to cancel without any charge
- How long it will take to get results
- The total cost you will pay
- Any guarantees

What if a credit repair company you hired does not live up to its promises? You have some options. You can:

- Sue them in federal court for your actual losses or for what you paid them, whichever is more

- Seek punitive damages – money to punish the company for violating the law
- Join other people in a class action lawsuit against the company, and if you win, the company has to pay your attorney's fees

Report Credit Repair Fraud

State Attorneys General

Many states also have laws regulating credit repair companies. If you have a problem with a credit repair company, report it to your local consumer affairs office or to your state attorney general (AG).

Federal Trade Commission

You also can file a complaint with the Federal Trade Commission. Although the FTC cannot resolve individual credit disputes, it can take action against a company if there is a pattern of possible law violations. File your complaint online at ftc.gov/complaint or call 877-FTC-HELP (877-382-4357).

Where to Get Legitimate Help

Just because you have a poor credit history does not mean you cannot get credit. Creditors set their own standards, and not all look at your credit history the same way. Some may look only at recent years to evaluate you for credit, and they may give you credit if your bill-paying history has improved. It may be worthwhile to contact creditors informally to discuss their credit standards.

If you are not disciplined enough to create a budget and stick to it, to work out a repayment plan with your creditors, or to keep track of your mounting bills, you might consider contacting a credit counseling organization. Many are nonprofit and work with you to solve your financial problems. But, remember that "nonprofit" status does not guarantee free, affordable, or even legitimate services. In fact, some credit counseling organizations – even some that claim nonprofit status – may charge high fees or hide their fees by pressuring people to make "voluntary" contributions that only cause more debt.

Most credit counselors offer services through local offices, online, or on the phone. If possible, find an organization that offers in-person counseling. Many universities, military bases, credit unions, housing authorities, and branches of the U.S. Cooperative Extension Service operate nonprofit credit counseling programs. Your financial institution, local consumer protection agency, and friends and family also may be good sources of information and referrals.

If you are thinking about filing for bankruptcy, be aware that bankruptcy laws require that you get credit counseling from a government-approved organization within six months before you file for bankruptcy relief. You can find a state-by-state list of government-approved organizations at www.usdoj.gov/ust, the website of the

U.S. Trustee Program. That is the organization within the U.S. Department of Justice (DOJ) that supervises bankruptcy cases and trustees. Be wary of credit counseling organizations that say they are government-approved, but do not appear on the list of approved organizations.

Reputable credit counseling organizations can advise you on managing your money and debts, help you develop a budget, and offer free educational materials and workshops. Their counselors are certified and trained in the areas of consumer credit, money and debt management, and budgeting. Counselors discuss your entire financial situation with you, and can help you develop a personalized plan to solve your money problems. An initial counseling session typically lasts an hour, with an offer of follow-up sessions.

CHAPTER 30

CHOOSING AND MANAGING A CREDIT CARD

About This Chapter: "Choosing and Managing a Credit Card," © 2021 Omnigraphics.

Credit cards are used in place of physical cash and are considered a convenient mode of payment. A credit card is a rectangular plastic or metal card that allows cardholders to borrow funds from the issuing bank or financial institution. Many businesses allow their customers to pay for their goods and services through credit cards, making a credit card payment convenient and universal. Credit cards are seemingly ideal for young adults who are starting to manage their finances. Credit cards have certain conditions, such as an applicable interest rate and additional charges paid back by the cardholder based on a billing plan. Some credit cards also offer a cash line of credit which means cardholders can access physical cash from ATMs and cash advances from credit card convenience checks. An essential aspect of credit cards is that they also come with a predetermined borrowing limit curated as per the card holder's credit rating or score.

Using a credit card is similar to taking a loan and is thus subject to interest charges charged to the card one month after the expenditure. Credit card companies must offer a minimum of 21 days which is called a "grace period," before interest is charged on the credit card. When purchasing with a credit card, the card's details are sent to the seller's bank, which then verifies your credit card with the credit card provider. Once verified, the provider can either approve or reject the transaction. If approved, money is deposited into the seller's account, and the same amount is deducted from the available credit balance in the credit card. At the end of the billing period, a statement of the transactions, and available credit is given to the card holder with details such as the minimum payment required and the due date for the same. In most cases, interest is not charged when the due is paid in full before the end of the grace period. A credit card has an annual percentage rate (APR) that reflects the expense of carrying a balance.

Types of Credit Cards

When choosing a credit card, there are various options ranging from basic credit cards to premium cards that offer additional advantages. It is essential to choose a credit card that adapts to one's financial needs and budget. Some common types of credit cards available are:

- Standard credit cards
- Student credit cards
- Charge cards
- Rewards credit cards
- Balance transfer credit cards
- Secured credit cards
- Subprime credit cards
- Prepaid credit cards
- Business credit cards
- Limited purpose cards

Benefits of a Credit Card

Credit cards are convenient and are among the best options during a medical emergency, while traveling, for unplanned expenses, and are also great at helping increase credit scores if used responsibly. Credit cards provide a variety of advantages and benefits such as:

- Earning rewards that can help reduce direct expenditures
- Increased purchase power
- Free from foreign transaction fees
- Help in securing a hotel room or car while traveling
- Free from checking or savings account charges
- Help improve credit scores

How to Choose a Credit Card

Before deciding on a credit card provider, there are some helpful points to remember, such as:

- **Considering the credit score.** Most credit card providers require cardholders to have at least five years of good credit history. The credit score depends on many factors such as income and debt history. One must have a good credit score before applying for a credit card.
- **Understanding expenditure.** It can help to have an idea of monthly or annual expenditure. This can help decide on a credit card that offers rewards for expenditures in areas of maximum spending. For example, if travel and groceries are the top areas of expenditure, one can choose a provider offering credit cards with rewards for purchasing airline tickets.

- **Knowledge of credit card terminology.** As young adults handling their own money, it can help to have a basic understanding of some standard terms that credit card providers use in their documents and promotions. Some terms include annual percentage rate (APR), minimum payments, perks, fees, rewards, and welcome bonus.
- **Checking for the need for a dedicated business credit card.** If there are expenses related to a self-owned business, it can help to have a separate business account and a dedicated credit card to help organize finances and in the event of a legal or tax audit.
- **Deciding on the most appropriate credit card.** After considerable research on the available types of credit cards, it can help choose one that fits the individual's financial requirements best regarding cashback and rewards. It is beneficial to select a credit card that offers a low APR or customized rewards since these are the best options for young adults and teenagers looking to choose a credit card.

When choosing between two or more competitive credit card providers, drawing up a comparison between them to come up with the best option can help. Some key points to look for when comparing credit cards are:

- APR for balance transfers, cash advances
- Annual fees
- Promotional APR terms and conditions
- Introductory bonus offer terms
- Rewards programs

How to Manage a Credit Card

Once a credit card is selected, the next step is to know how to handle the credit card responsibly. Using the credit card within limits will make it more of an asset than a financial burden in the long run.

- Use the credit card wisely for regular purchases that offer cashback and rewards. If done appropriately, one can earn or save a large sum of money. Use services that provide these returns on credit card payments and keep track of the money availed. Remember to spend within a budget and pay off the entire due at the end of the billing cycle to avoid losing earned rewards in interest payments.
- One can use the credit card to build a good credit score over time by ensuring that all dues are paid on time, and no penalties are levied. This can help in getting a quicker approval when a loan application is required in the future.
- Use the credit card to help organize spending behavior. When using the card regularly, one can also see spending patterns on the card and draw up

a better budget plan that will not push towards debt but will keep the cash flow running for the month.

- Keep the credit card as an emergency line of money for sudden expenditures that may arise. As a young adult or a college student without an emergency fund, one can use a credit card for minimal purchases to keep the card active and avoid being financially stranded.
- Protect the credit card with fraud and purchase protection. These cards are ultimately safer when compared to debit cards.

Credit Card Pitfalls to Avoid

Credit cards are a valuable tool in managing money and are beneficial to everyone. This does not take away from the fact that it is prone to risks and disadvantages. There are a few pitfalls that teenagers and young people interested in purchasing a credit card must avoid at all costs to help them manage their finances. Some of these mistakes are:

- Paying only the minimum amount. Paying the due in full and not just the minimum can help avoid carrying balances to the next billing cycle.
- Skipping a payment. Late payments can lower the credit score, especially if they are delayed by more than 30 days.
- Carrying forward a balance every month. This does more damage to the credit score and can lead to large sum payments at the end of the billing cycle.
- Making use of the cash advance facility. Cash advances on credit cards are chargeable with interest.
- No knowledge of APR and other fees. One must be aware of the rates and extra costs being levied to avoid excess debt.
- Using the entire credit limit
- Purchasing a credit card too often. This leads to an inquiry on the credit score and too many in a short period can lower the credit score.
- Closing a credit card account can reduce the length of credit history and also the credit score.
- Using the wrong card for a long time. Change the card according to your needs.
- Not utilizing rewards earned on credit card purchases

References

1. Luthi, Ben. "10 Mistakes You Are Probably Making with Your Credit Card," Money Under 30, February 8, 2021.
2. White, Alexandria. "10 Common Credit Card Mistakes You May Be Making and How to Avoid Them," Select, CNBC Network, August 25, 2020.
3. Weliver, David. "How to Use a Credit Card Responsibly," Money Under 30, October 19, 2020.

4. White, Alexandria. "How to Choose the Best Credit Card in 3 Easy Steps," Select, CNBC Network, February 1, 2021.
5. Black, Michelle. "How to Choose a Credit Card," The Points Guy, March 27, 2020.
6. Weliver, David. "How to Choose a Credit Card Wisely," Money Under 30, February 25, 2020.
7. "What Are the Advantages of Credit Cards?" Discover, March 18, 2020.
8. Irby, Latoya. "10 Types of Credit Cards, and How to Use Them," The Balance, July 21, 2020.
9. Lake, Rebecca. "How Do Credit Cards Work?" Investopedia, September 28, 2020.

CHAPTER 31

CREDIT CARD INTEREST RATE

About This Chapter: This chapter includes text excerpted from "What Is a Credit Card Interest Rate? What Does APR Mean?" Consumer Financial Protection Bureau (CFPB), July 12, 2017.

What Is a Credit Card Interest Rate? What Does Annual Percentage Rate Mean?

A credit card's interest rate is the price you pay for borrowing money.

For credit cards, the interest rates are typically stated as a yearly rate. This is called the "annual percentage rate" (APR). On most cards, you can avoid paying interest on purchases if you pay your balance in full each month by the due date.

You Paid Off Your Entire Bill When It Was Due Last Month and Still Got Charged Interest. How Can That Be?

If you have been carrying a balance, most card issuers will charge you interest from the time your bill was sent to you until the time your card issuer receives your payment. Different card issuers have different rules for determining when they charge interest. In general, once a card issuer begins to charge interest it will continue to do so until it receives your payment. This means that if you have been carrying a balance, you will be charged interest – sometimes called "residual interest" – from the time your bill was sent to you until the time your payment is received by your card issuer.

Your cardholder agreement should tell you the rules your card issuer applies. You should be able to find a copy of the agreement on your card issuer's website, and you can request a copy from your card issuer if it is not there.

What Is a Grace Period for a Credit Card?

A grace period is the period between the end of a billing cycle and the date your payment is due.

During this time, you may not be charged interest as long as you pay your balance in full by the due date. Credit card companies are not required to give a grace period. However, most credit cards provide a grace period on purchases.

If your card gives a grace period and you are not carrying a balance, then you can avoid paying interest on new purchases if you pay your balance in full by the due date. If you lose your grace period by not paying your balance in full by the due date, you will be charged interest on the unpaid portion of the balance. You will also be charged interest on purchases in the new billing cycle starting on the date each purchase is made.

Credit card companies must establish procedures to assure that their bills are mailed or delivered to you at least 21 days before the payment is due.

With credit cards, grace periods typically apply only to purchase transactions. If you use your card to get a cash advance or use a check you received from your card issuer, generally you must start paying interest as of the date of the transaction.

Tip: To keep your grace period, make sure to pay your bill in full each month and on time. If you pay in full some months, and not in other months, you may lose your grace period for the month that you do not pay in full and for the month after.

What Is a "Daily Periodic Rate" on a Credit Card?

Some card issuers calculate interest on the account using a daily periodic interest rate. A daily periodic interest rate generally is used to calculate interest by multiplying the rate by the amount owed at the end of each day.

This interest amount is then added to the previous day's balance, which means that interest is compounding on a daily basis.

However, the interest rate for a credit card is usually stated as an annual rate (the annual percentage rate or APR). The daily periodic interest rate generally can be calculated by dividing the annual percentage rate, or APR, by either 360 or 365, depending on the card issuer.

CHAPTER 32
UNDERSTANDING CREDIT CARD STATEMENT

About This Chapter: This chapter includes text excerpted from "Understand Your Credit Card Statement," MyCreditUnion.gov, February 19, 2010.

A credit card statement is a summary of how you have used your credit card for a billing period. If you have ever looked at credit card statements, you know how difficult they can be to read. Credit card statements are filled with terms, numbers and percentages that play a role in the calculation of your total credit card balance.

To be a responsible credit card user, it is important to read all the fine print and understand the numbers and terms on the statement. If you do not, you may end up with more credit card debt than you can handle.

It is also important to read your credit card statement carefully to spot any unauthorized charges or billing errors. Your liability for those charged may be limited if you report them in a timely manner.

1. Summary of Account Activity

A summary of the transactions on your account – your payments, credits, purchases, balance transfers, cash advances, fees, interest charges, and amounts past due. It will also show your new balance, available credit (your credit limit minus the amount you owe), and the last day of the billing period (payments or charges after this day will show up on your next bill).

2. Payment Information

Your total new balance, the minimum payment amount (the least amount you should pay), and the date your payment is due. A payment generally is considered on time if received by 5 p.m. on the day it is due. If mailed payments are not accepted on a due date (e.g., if the due date is on a weekend or holiday), the payment is considered on time if it arrives by 5. p.m. on the next business day.

Example: If your bill is due on July 4th and the credit card company does not receive mail that day, your payment will be on time if it arrives by mail by 5 p.m. on July 5th.

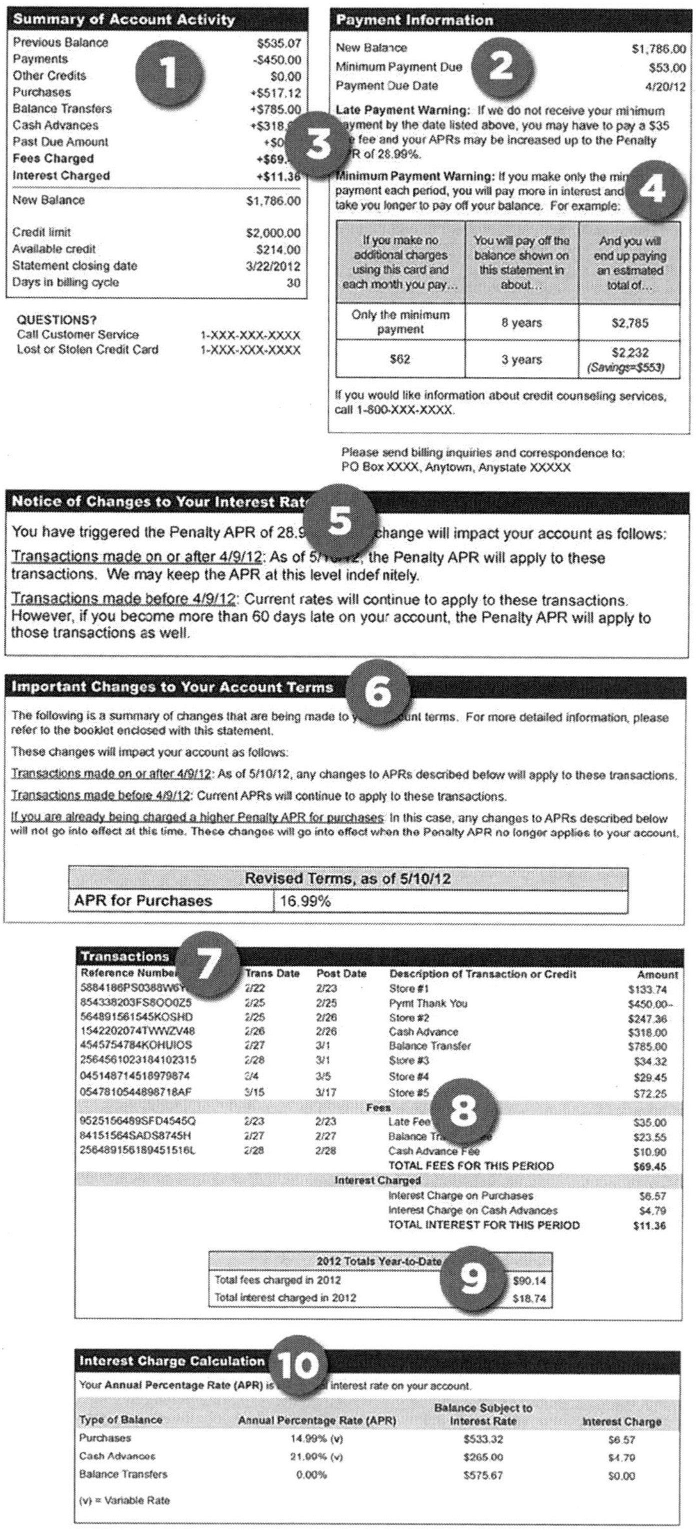

Summary of Account Activity

Previous Balance	$535.07
Payments	-$450.00
Other Credits	$0.00
Purchases	+$517.12
Balance Transfers	+$785.00
Cash Advances	+$318.
Past Due Amount	+$0
Fees Charged	**+$69.**
Interest Charged	**+$11.36**
New Balance	$1,786.00
Credit limit	$2,000.00
Available credit	$214.00
Statement closing date	3/22/2012
Days in billing cycle	30

QUESTIONS?
Call Customer Service 1-XXX-XXX-XXXX
Lost or Stolen Credit Card 1-XXX-XXX-XXXX

Payment Information

New Balance	$1,786.00
Minimum Payment Due	$53.00
Payment Due Date	4/20/12

Late Payment Warning: If we do not receive your minimum ayment by the date listed above, you may have to pay a $35 e fee and your APRs may be increased up to the Penalty R of 28.99%.

Minimum Payment Warning: If you make only the mi payment each period, you will pay more in interest and take you longer to pay off your balance. For example:

If you make no additional charges using this card and each month you pay...	You will pay off the balance shown on this statement in about...	And you will end up paying an estimated total of...
Only the minimum payment	8 years	$2,785
$62	3 years	$2,232 *(Savings=$553)*

If you would like information about credit counseling services, call 1-800-XXX-XXXX.

Please send billing inquiries and correspondence to:
PO Box XXXX, Anytown, Anystate XXXXX

Notice of Changes to Your Interest Rat

You have triggered the Penalty APR of 28.9 change will impact your account as follows:

Transactions made on or after 4/9/12: As of 5/ , the Penalty APR will apply to these transactions. We may keep the APR at this level indef nitely.

Transactions made before 4/9/12: Current rates will continue to apply to these transactions. However, if you become more than 60 days late on your account, the Penalty APR will apply to those transactions as well.

Important Changes to Your Account Terms

The following is a summary of changes that are being made to y unt terms. For more detailed information, please refer to the booklet enclosed with this statement.

These changes will impact your account as follows:

Transactions made on or after 4/9/12: As of 5/10/12, any changes to APRs described below will apply to these transactions.

Transactions made before 4/9/12: Current APRs will continue to apply to these transactions.

If you are already being charged a higher Penalty APR for purchases: In this case, any changes to APRs described below will not go into effect at this time. These changes will go into effect when the Penalty APR no longer applies to your account.

Revised Terms, as of 5/10/12	
APR for Purchases	16.99%

Transactions

Reference Numbe	Trans Date	Post Date	Description of Transaction or Credit	Amount
5884186PS0388W6Y	2/22	2/23	Store #1	$133.74
854338203FS8OO0Z5	2/25	2/25	Pymt Thank You	$450.00-
564891561545KOSHD	2/25	2/26	Store #2	$247.36
1542202074TWWZV48	2/26	2/26	Cash Advance	$318.00
4545754784KOHUIOS	2/27	3/1	Balance Transfer	$785.00
2564561023184102315	2/28	3/1	Store #3	$34.32
045148714518979874	3/4	3/5	Store #4	$29.45
05478105448987 18AF	3/15	3/17	Store #5	$72.25
			Fees	
9525156489SFD4545Q	2/23	2/23	Late Fee	$35.00
84151564SADS8745H	2/27	2/27	Balance Tr	$23.55
256489156189451516L	2/28	2/28	Cash Advance Fee	$10.90
			TOTAL FEES FOR THIS PERIOD	**$69.45**
			Interest Charged	
			Interest Charge on Purchases	$6.57
			Interest Charge on Cash Advances	$4.79
			TOTAL INTEREST FOR THIS PERIOD	**$11.36**

2012 Totals Year-to-Date	
Total fees charged in 2012	$90.14
Total interest charged in 2012	$18.74

Interest Charge Calculation

Your **Annual Percentage Rate (APR)** is interest rate on your account.

Type of Balance	Annual Percentage Rate (APR)	Balance Subject to Interest Rate	Interest Charge
Purchases	14.99% (v)	$533.32	$6.57
Cash Advances	21.99% (v)	$265.00	$4.79
Balance Transfers	0.00%	$575.67	$0.00

(v) = Variable Rate

Figure 32.1. Sample Credit Card Statement

3. Late Payment Warning

This section states any additional fees and the higher interest rate that may be charged if your payment is late.

4. Minimum Payment Warning

An estimate of how long it can take to pay off your credit card balance if you make only the minimum payment each month, and an estimate of how much you likely will pay, including interest, in order to pay off your bill in three years (assuming you have no additional charges).

5. Notice of Changes to Your Interest Rates

If you trigger the penalty rate (e.g., by going over your credit limit or paying your bill late), your credit card company may notify you that your rates will be increasing. The credit card company must tell you at least 45 days before your rates change.

6. Other Changes to Your Account Terms

If your credit card company is going to raise interest rates or fees or make other significant changes to your account, it must notify you at least 45 days before the changes take effect.

7. Transactions

A list of all the transactions that have occurred since your last statement (purchases, payments, credits, cash advances, and balance transfers). Some credit card companies group them by type of transactions. Others list them by date of transaction or by user, if there are different users on the account. Review the list carefully to make sure that you recognize all of the transactions. This is the section of your statement where you can check for unauthorized transactions or other problems.

8. Fees and Interest Charges

Credit card companies must list the fees and interest charges separately on your monthly bill. Interest charges must be listed by type of transaction (e.g., you may be charged a different interest rate for purchases than for cash advances).

9. Year-to-Date Totals

The total that you have paid in fees and interest charges for the current year. You can avoid some fees, such as over-the-limit fees, by managing how much you charge, and by paying on time to avoid late payment fees.

10. Interest Charge Calculation

A summary of the interest rates on the different types of transactions, account balances, the amount of each, and the interest charged for each type of transaction.

CHAPTER 33

PROBLEMS RESULTING FROM MINIMUM PAYMENTS WITH HIGH-INTEREST RATES

What Is a Minimum Credit Card Payment?

A minimum credit card payment is the lowest amount paid on a balance statement. When the minimum payment is paid on time, you are fulfilling your obligation as a cardholder and helping to build a favorable payment history on your credit report.

Credit card issuers charge you interest for the privilege of borrowing money and this process is usually represented as the annual percentage rate (APR). Most credit cards feature variable APRs that change in response to the prime rate (rate of interest). For example, if the prime rate is 4 percent and your credit card company charges a prime rate plus 12 percent, the APR will be 16 percent.

Making only the bare minimum monthly payments on your credit cards might cause you grief. By paying only the minimum amount due each month, you extend the time it takes to pay off your credit card debt and pay significantly more interest than you would otherwise.

How the Minimum Credit Card Payment Is Calculated

Flat Percentage

Some credit card issuers, such as credit unions and subprime lenders (those who provide credit cards to people with lower credit scores), calculate the minimum monthly payment for your credit card using a flat percentage.

In this scenario, the minimum payment on a credit card is calculated using the total balance on the cardholder's account, including financing charges and any fees.

Monthly minimum payments on credit cards with a fixed percentage minimum payment, range from 2 percent to 4 percent of your debt. With that in mind, if your total credit card amount is $3,000 and the flat rate is 2 percent, your minimum monthly payment would be $60.

Formula to Calculate the Payments

Some credit card issuers calculate the minimum payment by dividing your entire debt by a percentage, excluding interest and fees. The interest and fees are then added to the minimum balance payable.

If the minimum payment percentage calculation is 1 percent of your outstanding balance, a debt of $1,250 with a 16-percent interest rate would have a minimum payment of $29.17. The 1 percent is $12.50, and the interest is $16.67 (monthly), adding up to a total of $29.17.

Making Only Minimum Payment

While it is necessary to make at least the minimum payment, carrying a balance from month to month is not a good idea since you will accrue interest and risk going into debt.

Card issuers are required by law to include a "minimum payment warning" on each billing statement under the Credit Card Accountability, Responsibility, and Disclosure (CARD) Act of 2009. This is frequently depicted by a chart that shows the time it will take to pay off your balance as well as the total amount you will pay (including interest) if you only pay the minimum.

Missing the Minimum Payment

Your credit card issuer might charge you a late fee if you miss your monthly minimum payment or pay less than the minimum.

- If you miss a minimum payment, you may lose any promotional interest rate you have on your account. Your credit card issuer may also raise the interest rate to the penalty rate if you miss two minimum payments in a row.
- The credit card issuer will report the late payment to the credit bureaus if you are more than 30 days late on your minimum payment. This missed payment will be published on your credit report for seven years. Your credit score may be damaged as well, particularly in the months following the late payment.

Payments that have been missed in the past will increase the current minimum payment required. Not only will you be forced to make current and missed minimum payments, but a late charge will be applied to the total amount to reinstate your account. Because the minimum amount increases with each missed payment, catching up on your payments becomes more difficult.

Minimum Payment and Credit Score

A good credit score is measured by credit usage, the quantity of credit available against the credit used, which should account for 30 percent on the Fair Isaac Corporation (FICO) score.

Whether you are making minimum payments or not, your outstanding credit card balances should be kept at or below 30 percent of your credit limits. For example, if the total credit limit on all your cards is $6,000, your outstanding balances should be $1,800 or less.

If your credit card balance amount is more than 30 percent of your credit card limits, your credit score will reduce. Making just the minimum payment will result in your debt growing exponentially, which will then take years to repay.

References

1. Irby, Latoya. "Credit Card Minimum Payment Calculation," The Balance, July 30, 2020.
2. Egan, John; Kissell, Chris. "Is It OK to Make Minimum Payments on Credit Cards?" U.S. News and World Report, November 12, 2019.
3. White, Alexandria. "Here's What Happens If You Only Pay the Minimum on Your Credit Card," CNBC, May 5, 2021.
4. "Understanding Credit Card Interest," Investopedia, March 1, 2021.

PART 5 | STAYING OUT OF DEBT

CHAPTER 34
LOAN OPTIONS FOR PEOPLE UNDER 18

When you are younger than 18, it can be difficult to get a loan approved, but it is not impossible. When a loan provider does a credit check on you, they will be assessing their risk and, in particular, checking to determine how likely it is that you will be able to repay the loan. However, because of your age, the lender may find it hard to judge how reliable you might be.

There are many reasons why a young person may opt for a loan. They might, for example, want to get a loan to buy their first car or to fund their studies. Other reasons include buying a house, going on a vacation, paying for a wedding, or paying off debts.

Types of Loans for Young People

There is a prime age set for borrowing based on the risk factors that age carries. To put it simply, the older you are, the less time you will have to repay your debt and the younger you are, the less income and experience you will have to indicate the likelihood that you will repay your debt. Despite these obstacles, a person younger than 18 can be eligible for certain types of loans. Some of these are listed below:

Personal Loans

If you are under 18 with little credit history, then you may be eligible for a personal loan. However, the amount that you are offered might be less, or at a higher rate of interest than advertised. This is because the lender may consider a person below the age of 18 to be a potentially risky prospect.

It is also important to note that your credit score drops each time you apply for a loan, so applying for many is unwise and a lower credit score will make it difficult to get a loan or credit product in the future.

Search tools, such as insurance.com, etc., allow you to see whether you are eligible for a loan. Since rejection of a loan adversely affects your credit score, it is always better to take advantage of online tools such as these.

Student Loans

There are three types of student loans:

- Federal loans
- Private loans
- Refinance loans (once you leave school)

Federal loans are funded by the government, while private and refinanced loans are provided by banks, credit unions, and states. Federal loans are more flexible than private loans. However, the loan that is best suited to you will be determined by several factors, including your financial need, grade point average (GPA), and credit history.

A "Free Application for Federal Student Aid" (FAFSA) application must be filled out in order to get a federal loan. A borrower usually must apply with the bank or financial institution directly for private or refinanced loans.

Cosigner Loans

Since few people under the age of 18 will be approved for a loan, they may wish to consider asking their parents, relatives, or even an older friend to be a guarantor for them. This person takes on the responsibility of repaying the loan if the borrower is unable to pay it.

Learn to Explore Loan Choices

As soon as you know your budget, shop around. Banks, credit unions, and other lenders are common places to get preapproved. Comparing offers will help you get the loan that is right for you.

(Source: "Learn to Explore Loan Choices," Consumer Financial Protection Bureau (CFPB).)

Alternatives to Loans

There are other options that a person can consider before taking out a loan. Some of the options are listed below:

Check with Peers

Even though peers may not always have money they can lend, they may be able to direct you to someone who can help. Hence, checking with peers is always worth the effort.

Check with Family

If a family member or close friend is able to lend money to you, then you may wish to consider asking them. However, it is also important to remember that even if the money is being borrowed from a person of trust, it is recommended that you draw up a contract that lists details about the repayment amount, loan period, and whether or not interest will be paid on the loan.

Government Support

People who receive federal benefits may be eligible for an interest-free loan that can be used for everyday essentials such as rent; therefore, check your eligibility for such benefits.

Credit Cards

Interest-free credit cards can be used as an alternative to a loan. However, it is important to note when the interest-free period ends, or you could end up paying interest that is higher than the typical interest rate on payments made after the interest-free period ends.

Savings

If the loan is desire in order to purchase a car or move out, then start saving for the expense as early as possible. This could result in not having to take out a loan at all.

Tips for Getting a Loan at 18

Here are some suggestions to consider if you are 18 and trying to get a loan:

- Show evidence that you can save.
- Offer collateral.
- Get a letter of recommendation and/or proof of employment from your employer if employed.
- Apply for a lower amount.
- Opt for a secured loan.

Taking out a loan at a young age can give you access to quick funds and help you build a credit history, but it may come with certain negative consequences such as a high-interest rate and an increased risk of defaulting on your payment. Hence, it is always important to think of alternative ways to raise the funds before you choose to pursue a loan. Finally, if you are considering a loan, make sure you can afford to repay it.

References

1. "Loans for Young People," GoCompare, January 17, 2016.
2. "Compare Loans for 18-Year-Olds," Finder, January 5, 2020.
3. "Types of Student Loans: Which Is Best for You?" NerdWallet, June 13, 2019.

CHAPTER 35
UNDERSTANDING COMPOUND INTEREST

An interest rate is the percentage of a principal amount, either charged by the lender for the usage of its funds or products, or the amount received from the bank for a particular investment. The lent sum is referred to as the "principal." An interest rate is usually split into two categories, such as simple interest and compound interest.

When evaluating a loan's terms, the interest rate is not the only aspect that has to be considered. Even if two loans have the same principal amounts, interest rates, and repayment terms, the amount of interest a person pays might vary greatly, especially if one loan applies simple interest and the other applies compound interest.

Simple Interest

The principal balance of the loan is used to compute simple interest. Simple interest is a fixed percentage of the principal amount borrowed or lent that is paid or received over a period.

Compound Interest

Compound interest is when the interest amount is added to the principal amount invested or borrowed and the interest rate is applied to the new higher rate. It is just interest on interest, which leads to an exponential increase over time.

When it comes to money management, compound interest is a must-know concept. It can either help in making a larger return on savings and investments or also work against a person when she or he has taken a loan.

How Compound Interest Works

Assume you deposit $1,000 in a savings account with a 10-percent annual interest rate. You will have $1,100 at the end of the first year, which includes the $1,000 investment plus $100 in interest. That $100 represents "simple" interest or interest calculated just on the principal invested.

You will have \$1,210 at the end of the second year, which includes the \$1,100 from the previous year plus \$110 in additional interest (10 percent of \$1,100).

Calculating Compound Interest

Compound interest incurs at a rate determined by the frequency of compounding – the higher the number of compounding periods, the higher the compound interest rate. The formula to calculate compound interest rate is:

$A = P(1+r/n)^{nt}$

- P is the principal
- r is the annual interest rate
- n is how often the interest compounds annually
- t is the time or total number of years
- A is the total amount you will wind up with at the end of the tenure

A Quick Calculation

You have \$1,000 that is compounded monthly at 5 percent. After a period of 15 years, what will be the amount of money you have?

$A = P\{1 + (r/n)\}^{nt}$

- A = 1000 (1 + [.05 / 12]) 12 x 15
- A = 1000 (1.0041666...) 180
- A = 1000 (2.113703)
- A = 2113.70

You will have approximately \$2,114 after 15 years. The \$1,000 represents your initial contribution, while the \$1,114 represents interest.

> Knowing how quickly your investment will double in value can help you determine a "ballpark" estimate of your investment's future value over a long period of time.
>
> *(Source: "Tips for Teaching Students about Saving and Investing," U.S. Securities and Exchange Commission (SEC).)*

How Compound Interest Rates Affect Debts

On average daily balances, many credit cards accrue interest every day. While the math may be difficult, the concept is simple – when you carry a balance from month to month, compound interest adds to your debt. Paying off credit card debt can be challenging due to the (sometimes, high) interest rate and daily compounding, which is why you should always aim to pay off your credit card amount in full each month. You will pay no interest and will not have to worry about accumulating interest on your loan this way.

If your monthly payment does not cover the monthly interest, negative amortization occurs, and your debt grows. If you add the unpaid interest to your principal debt amount, the interest rate will be applied to the greater sum.

Why Compound Interest Is Powerful

Frequency

Compounding periods that are more frequent – daily, for example – produce better outcomes. Look for accounts that compound regularly when creating a savings account. Although you may only see interest payments deposited to your account once a month, computations can be done daily.

Time

Compounding has an effect over time. When money is left untouched to grow, you have a bigger number of computations or "credits" to the account.

Interest Rates

The interest rate on your account also plays a significant role in the long-term balance of your account. Higher rates represent a faster growth rate, although compound interest can compensate for a lower amount. An account compounding at a lesser rate might end up with a bigger balance than an account employing a simple interest, especially over a long tenure.

Deposits

Your account balance may be affected by withdrawals and deposits. It is ideal to let your money grow or to make regular contributions to your account. When you take money out of your account, the compounding impact is reduced.

References

1. DeNicola, Louis. "How Does Compound Interest Work?" Experian, September 16, 2019.
2. Depersio, Greg. "Simple Interest vs Compound Interest: What Is the Difference?" Investopedia, April 5, 2021.
3. Fernando, Jason. "Compound Interest," Investopedia, February 16, 2021.
4. Pritchard, Justin. "What Is Compound Interest" The Balance, May 9, 2021.

CHAPTER 36
PROBLEMS ASSOCIATED WITH DEBT

About This Chapter: "Problems Associated with Debt," © 2021 Omnigraphics.

The term "debt" refers to an amount of money owed by a person or an organization to another. A person can lend money to another person at a set or variable interest rate. As a result, the borrower will repay both the principal and the interest throughout the course of the loan payback period.

Mortgage loans, vehicle loans, credit card debt, and income taxes are the common kinds of debt owed by families and individuals. Individual debt is a means for people to spend an expected income paired with future purchasing, rather than waiting to earn the same.

Good Debt versus Bad Debt

Good Debt

Money due for items that might assist in developing wealth or boost income over time, such as education loans, mortgages, or a business loan, is referred to as "good" debt. A few things worth being in debt are:

- **Education.** In general, the higher one's educational attainment, the higher their earning potential is. Education also has a favorable impact on one's capacity to find work. Workers with a higher level of education are more likely to be hired in well-paying positions.
- **Business development.** Borrowing money to establish your own business falls under the category of good debt.
- **Housing or real estate.** Housing loans are taken to construct or purchase a property. People can live in it for a few years, and then sell it for a profit. Residential real estate can also be rented out to earn revenue.

Bad Debt

Credit cards and other consumer debt are examples of "bad" debt. Borrowing money to buy quickly depreciating assets or for the sole purpose of consuming is considered bad debt. A few things you should avoid getting into debt are:

- **Vehicles.** While you may find it hard to live without a vehicle, borrowing money to purchase one is not a good financial decision. The vehicle will start depreciating immediately after buying it from the auto dealership.
- **Apparels.** Clothing is frequently stated to be worth less than half of what buyers spend for them. Using a high-interest credit card to purchase them is not a sensible use of debt.

Debt Crisis

A debt crisis occurs when a government (for e.g., country, state, province, county, or city) is unable to repay its debts. When a government's expenditures exceed for an extended period, the country may face a debt crisis. Though a debt crisis is usually a national-level situation, an individual can also experience it.

Student Loan Debt

For many people, student loans make up a big portion of the debt they owe. Sometimes people borrow more than they will be able to afford given the likely pay they will earn in their profession. Sometimes people get into trouble because they do not understand the terms of their loans and the consequences of letting interest build up.

(Source: "A Financial Empowerment Toolkit for Community Volunteers," Consumer Financial Protection Bureau (CFPB).)

Household Debt Crisis

When a family falls behind on their monthly payments, it enters a household financial crisis. Household debt may be divided into three categories:

- Home mortgages
- Credit card debt (also called "revolving credit")
- Auto, furniture, and college loans (also known as "nonrevolving credit")

Reasons for a Household Debt Crisis

A household debt crisis might be triggered by a sudden loss of income or an increase in expenditure. Medical bills are the leading cause of bankruptcy in the United States, accounting for half of all bankruptcies. Other factors include long periods of unemployment or losses that are not covered by insurance.

Overcoming Household Debt Crisis

Firstly, your income should be increased by getting a second job, getting a raise or promotion, working part-time, or selling assets, such as your home or property. Secondly, your total spending must be reduced. Switching to a lower-interest credit card, paying cash instead of credit, and paying extra on your debt are all options.

Business Debt Crisis

When an industry or organization has problems repaying its bonds, it is said to be in a corporate debt crisis. They may be rated as a bad investment. When this happens, issuing new bonds becomes more expensive for the corporation.

Causes of a Business Debt Crisis

Debt problems in businesses are caused by a variety of circumstances. Many small-scale industries end up with heavy debt, as they might not have the proper funding or management skills in the initial years of their business. At times, a company's business plan may be imperfect or its product may lack a strong competitive edge.

Overcoming Business Debt Crisis

Before agreeing to cut payments, lenders might choose new management. If the economy is in a crisis, the corporation may need to decrease expenses and enhance customer service. It is possible to engage a turnaround consultant who may help uncover better business models and strategies.

Why Debt Is Bad

Though a small amount of debt incurred using a credit card can seem harmless, it is the gateway to end up reaching thousands of dollars in debt. The major problems that debts can cause in a person's life are:

- Debt is an actual process of borrowing your future income and unknowingly, you spend more than what you need.
- You end up spending more than the actual amount, in the form of interest once a credit card is swiped or a loan is taken.
- Having a huge outstanding balance on your credit card, pending education loan installments, or a vehicle loan with a higher debt amount may lead to the rejection of a home loan.
- It is difficult not to be concerned about how you will make your payments or avoid taking on additional debt to make ends meet while you already are in debt. Debt-related stress may cause a variety of health issues, including migraines, anxiety, depression, and even heart attacks.
- Debt puts undue strain on one's household finances and can leave your spouse and children without financial stability, which can, later, lead to marital problems.
- The amount of debt you hold should preferably account for 30 percent of your credit score. This credit score will deteriorate if you have more debt than your credit limit.

References

1. Amadeo, Kimberly. "Debt Crisis Causes and Cures," The Balance, April 27, 2021.

2. Smith, Lisa. "Good Debt versus Bad Debt: An Overview," Investopedia, April 29, 2021.
3. Alvarez, Janet. "Good Debt versus Bad Debt: Why What You Have Been Told Is Probably Wrong," Consumer News and Business Channel (CNBC), July 20, 2020.
4. Irby, Latora. "9 Reasons Debt Is Bad for You," The Balance, September 29, 2020.

CHAPTER 37
SEEKING CREDIT COUNSELING

About This Chapter: This chapter includes text excerpted from "What Is Credit Counseling?" Consumer Financial Protection Bureau (CFPB), February 2, 2018.

What Is Credit Counseling?

Credit counseling organizations can advise you on your money and debts, help you with a budget, and offer money management workshops.

Credit counseling organizations are usually nonprofit organizations. Typically, their counselors are certified and trained in the areas of consumer credit, money and debt management, and budgeting. Counselors discuss your financial situation with you and help you develop a personalized plan to solve your money problems. Here are some examples of what credit counselors might do:

- Advise you on managing your money and debts
- Help you develop a budget
- Help you get a copy of your credit report and scores
- May offer free educational materials and workshops
- Organize a "debt management plan" to pay down your debts

Tip: If you are having trouble making payments on your debts, a credit counselor may be able to help you with advice or by organizing a "debt management plan" for all your debts. Typically, under a debt management plan you make a single payment to the credit counseling organization each month or pay period and the credit counseling organization makes monthly payments to each of your creditors. Under debt management plans, credit counselors usually do not negotiate any reduction in the amounts you owe – instead, they can lower your overall monthly payment. They do so by negotiating extensions of the periods over which you can repay a loan and by asking creditors to lower the interest rates and waive certain fees.

How Do You Find a Credit Counselor?

Most credit counselors offer services through in-person meetings at local offices, the Internet, or on the telephone. To get started, you can try the Financial Counseling

Association of America, on their website (fcaa.org) or by phone at 800-450-1794, or the National Foundation for Credit Counseling, on their website (www.nfcc.org) or by phone at 800-388-2227.

Once you have developed a list of potential credit counseling organizations, check them out with your state attorney general (www.naag.org/current-attorneys-general.php) and state consumer protection agency (www.usa.gov/state-consumer). Ask the counselors for free information about their services.

How Do You Choose Which Credit Counselor Is Right for You?

A reputable credit counseling organization should be willing to send you free information about itself and the services it provides without requiring you to provide any details about your situation. If a service does not do that, consider this a red flag and go elsewhere for help.

Here are some questions to ask to help you find the best credit counseling service for you:

What Services Do You Offer?

Look for an organization that offers a range of services, including budget counseling and classes for managing spending and debt. Avoid organizations that push a debt management plan as your only option before they have spent a significant amount of time analyzing your financial situation.

How Is Credit Counseling Offered?

Services may be offered in-person, by phone, or online. An initial counseling session typically lasts an hour, with an offer of follow-up sessions.

What Are Your Fees?

Are there set-up or monthly fees? Get a specific price quote in writing. Although most credit counseling organizations are nonprofits, credit counselors may charge fees for some of their services that they take out of the payments you make to them.

What If I Cannot Afford to Pay the Fees or Make Contributions?

If an organization would not help you because you cannot afford to pay, look elsewhere.

Will You Have a Formal Written Agreement or Contract with Me?

Do not sign anything without reading it first. Make sure all verbal promises are also in writing. As with any contract, do not sign anything that you do not understand.

What Are the Counselor's Qualifications?

Is the organization or counselor accredited or certified? What are the qualifications of its credit counselors? Find out about what training or professional certifications the counselor has received.

How Are Your Employees Paid?

Are the employees paid more if you sign up for certain services, if you pay a fee, or if you make a contribution to your organization? If the answer is yes, consider this a red flag and go elsewhere.

CHAPTER 38
DEALING WITH DEBT

About This Chapter: This chapter includes text excerpted from "Coping with Debt," Federal Trade Commission (FTC), November 2012.

Having trouble paying your bills? Getting dunning notices from creditors? Are your accounts being turned over to debt collectors? Are you worried about losing your home or your car? You are not alone. Many people face a financial crisis at some point in their lives. Whether the crisis is caused by personal or family illness, the loss of a job, or overspending, it can seem overwhelming. But, often, it can be overcome. Your financial situation does not have to go from bad to worse.

If you or someone you know is in financial hot water, consider these options: self-help using realistic budgeting and other techniques; debt relief services, such as credit counseling or debt settlement from a reputable organization; debt consolidation; or bankruptcy. How do you know which will work best for you? It depends on your level of debt, your level of discipline, and your prospects for the future.

Self-Help

Developing a Budget

The first step toward taking control of your financial situation is to do a realistic assessment of how much money you take in and how much money you spend. Start by listing your income from all sources. Then, list your "fixed" expenses – those that are the same each month – such as mortgage payments or rent, car payments, and insurance premiums. Next, list the expenses that vary – such as groceries, entertainment, and clothing. Writing down all your expenses, even those that seem insignificant, is a helpful way to track your spending patterns, identify necessary expenses, and prioritize the rest. The goal is to make sure you can make ends meet on the basics: housing, food, healthcare, insurance, and education. You can find information about budgeting and money management techniques online, at your public library, and in bookstores. Computer software programs can be useful tools for developing and maintaining a budget, balancing your checkbook, and creating plans to save money and pay down your debt.

Contacting Your Creditors

Contact your creditors immediately if you are having trouble making ends meet. Tell them why it is difficult for you, and try to work out a modified payment plan that reduces your payments to a more manageable level. Do not wait until your accounts have been turned over to a debt collector. At that point, your creditors have given up on you.

Dealing with Debt Collectors

Federal law dictates how and when a debt collector may contact you: not before 8 a.m., after 9 p.m., or while you are at work if the collector knows that your employer does not approve of the calls. Collectors may not harass you, lie, or use unfair practices when they try to collect a debt. And they must honor a written request from you to stop further contact.

Managing Your Auto and Home Loans

Your debts can be unsecured or secured. Secured debts usually are tied to an asset, such as your car for a car loan, or your house for a mortgage. If you stop making payments, lenders can repossess your car or foreclose on your house. Unsecured debts are not tied to any particular asset, and include most credit card debt, bills for medical care, and signature loans.

Most automobile financing agreements allow a creditor to repossess your car any time you are in default. No notice is required. If your car is repossessed, you may have to pay the balance due on the loan, as well as towing and storage costs, to get it back. If you cannot do this, the creditor may sell the car. If you see default approaching, you may be better off selling the car yourself and paying off the debt: You will avoid the added costs of repossession and a negative entry on your credit report.

If you fall behind on your mortgage, contact your lender immediately to avoid foreclosure. Most lenders are willing to work with you if they believe you are acting in good faith and the situation is temporary. Some lenders may reduce or suspend your payments for a short time. When you resume regular payments, though, you may have to pay an additional amount toward the past due total. Other lenders may agree to change the terms of the mortgage by extending the repayment period to reduce the monthly debt. Ask whether additional fees would be assessed for these changes, and calculate how much they total in the long term.

If you and your lender cannot work out a plan, contact a housing counseling agency. Some agencies limit their counseling services to homeowners with FHA mortgages, but many offer free help to any homeowner who is having trouble making mortgage payments. Call the local office of the Department of Housing and Urban Development or the housing authority in your state, city, or county for help in finding a legitimate housing counseling agency near you.

Debt Relief Services

If you are struggling with significant credit card debt, and cannot work out a repayment plan with your creditors on your own, consider contacting a debt relief service such as credit counseling or debt settlement. Depending on the type of service, you might get advice on how to deal with your mounting bills or create a plan for repaying your creditors.

Before you do business with any debt relief service, check it out with your state Attorney General and local consumer protection agency. They can tell you if any consumer complaints are on file about the firm you are considering doing business with. Ask your state Attorney General if the company is required to be licensed to work in your state and, if so, whether it is.

If you are thinking about getting help to stabilize your financial situation, do some homework first. Find out what services a business provides, how much it costs, and how long it may take to get the results they promised. Do not rely on verbal promises. Get everything in writing, and read your contracts carefully.

Credit Counseling

Reputable credit counseling organizations can advise you on managing your money and debts, help you develop a budget, and offer free educational materials and workshops. Their counselors are certified and trained in consumer credit, money and debt management, and budgeting. Counselors discuss your entire financial situation with you, and help you develop a personalized plan to solve your money problems. An initial counseling session typically lasts an hour, with an offer of follow-up sessions.

Most reputable credit counselors are nonprofits and offer services through local offices, online, or on the phone. If possible, find an organization that offers in-person counseling. Many universities, military bases, credit unions, housing authorities, and branches of the U.S. Cooperative Extension Service operate nonprofit credit counseling programs. Your financial institution, local consumer protection agency, and friends and family also may be good sources of information and referrals.

But, be aware that "nonprofit" status does not guarantee that services are free, affordable, or even legitimate. In fact, some credit counseling organizations charge high fees, which they may hide, or urge their clients to make "voluntary" contributions that can cause more debt.

Debt Management Plans

If your financial problems stem from too much debt or your inability to repay your debts, a credit counseling agency may recommend that you enroll in a debt management plan (DMP). A DMP alone is not credit counseling, and DMPs are not for everyone. Do not sign up for one of these plans unless and until a certified credit counselor has spent time thoroughly reviewing your financial situation, and has offered you customized advice on managing your money. Even if a DMP is appropriate for you, a reputable credit counseling organization still can help you create a budget and teach you money management skills.

In a DMP, you deposit money each month with the credit counseling organization. It uses your deposits to pay your unsecured debts, such as your credit card bills, student loans, and medical bills, according to a payment schedule the counselor develops with you and your creditors. Your creditors may agree to lower your interest rates or waive certain fees. But, it is a good idea to check with all your creditors to be sure they offer the concessions that a credit counseling organization describes to you. A successful DMP requires you to make regular, timely payments; it could take 48 months or more to complete your DMP. Ask the credit counselor to estimate how long it will take for you to complete the plan. You may have to agree not to apply for – or use – any additional credit while you are participating in the plan.

Debt Settlement Programs

Debt settlement programs typically are offered by for-profit companies, and involve them negotiating with your creditors to allow you to pay a "settlement" to resolve your debt – a lump sum that is less than the full amount that you owe. To make that lump sum payment, the program asks that you set aside a specific amount of money every month in savings. Debt settlement companies usually ask that you transfer this amount every month into an escrow-like account to accumulate enough savings to pay off any settlement that is eventually reached. Further, these programs often encourage or instruct their clients to stop making any monthly payments to their creditors.

Debt Settlement Has Risks

Although a debt settlement company may be able to settle one or more of your debts, there are risks associated with these programs to consider before enrolling:

- These programs often require that you deposit money in a special savings account for 36 months or more before all your debts will be settled. Many people have trouble making these payments long enough to get all (or even some) of their debts settled, and end up dropping out the programs as a result. Before you sign up for a debt settlement program, review your budget carefully to make sure you are financially capable of setting aside the required monthly amounts for the full length of the program.
- Your creditors have no obligation to agree to negotiate a settlement of the amount you owe. So there is a possibility that your debt settlement company will not be able to settle some of your debts – even if you set aside the monthly amounts required by the program. Also, debt settlement companies often try to negotiate smaller debts first, leaving interest and fees on large debts to continue to mount.

- Because debt settlement programs often ask or encourage you to stop sending payments directly to your creditors, they may have a negative impact on your credit report and other serious consequences. For example, your debts may continue to accrue late fees and penalties that can put you further in the hole. You also may get calls from your creditors or debt collectors requesting repayment. You could even be sued for repayment. In some instances, when creditors win a lawsuit, they have the right to garnish your wages or put a lien on your home.

Debt Settlement and Debt Elimination Scams

Some companies offering debt settlement programs may not deliver on their promises, like their "guarantees" to settle all your credit card debts for 30 to 60 percent of the amount you owe. Other companies may try to collect their fees from you before they settle any of your debts. The FTC's Telemarketing Sales Rule prohibits companies that sell debt settlement and other debt relief services on the phone from charging a fee before they settle or reduce your debt. Some companies may not explain the risks associated with their programs, including that many (or most) of their clients drop out without settling their debts, that their clients' credit reports may suffer, or that debt collectors may continue to call them.

Before you enroll in a debt settlement program, do your homework. You are making a big decision that involves spending a lot of your money that could go toward paying down your debt. Enter the name of the company name with the word "complaints" into a search engine. Read what others have said about the companies you are considering, including whether they are involved in a lawsuit with any state or federal regulators for engaging in deceptive or unfair practices.

Fees

If you do business with a debt settlement company, you may have to put money in a dedicated bank account, which will be administered by an independent third party. The funds are yours and you are entitled to the interest that accrues. The account administrator may charge you a reasonable fee for account maintenance, and is responsible for transferring funds from your account to pay your creditors and the debt settlement company when settlements occur.

Disclosure Requirements

Before you sign up for the service, the debt relief company must give you information about the program:

- **Price and terms.** The company must explain its fees and any conditions on its services.
- **Results.** The company must tell you how long it will take to get results – how many months or years before it will make an offer to each creditor for a settlement.

- **Offers.** The company must tell you how much money or what percentage of each outstanding debt you must save before it will make an offer to each creditor on your behalf.
- **Nonpayment.** If the company asks you to stop making payments to your creditors – or if the program relies on your not making payments – it must tell you about the possible negative consequences of your action.

The debt relief company also must tell you:
- That the funds are yours and you are entitled to the interest earned
- The account administrator is not affiliated with the debt relief provider and does not get referral fees
- That you may withdraw your money at any time without penalty

Tax Consequences

Depending on your financial condition, any savings you get from debt relief services can be considered income and taxable. Credit card companies and others may report settled debt to the IRS, which the IRS considers income, unless you are "insolvent." Insolvency is when your total debts are more than the fair market value of your total assets. Insolvency can be complex to determine. Talk to a tax professional if are not sure whether you qualify for this exception.

How to Spot Fake Debt Collectors

Not everyone who calls saying that you owe a debt is a real debt collector. Some are scammers who are just trying to take your money. So how can you tell?

A caller may be a fake debt collector if they:
- Want you to repay a debt you do not recognize
- Refuse to give you their mailing address or phone number
- Pressure you, or try to scare you into paying by threatening to report you to law enforcement or have you arrested

(Source: "Fake and Abusive Debt Collectors," Federal Trade Commission (FTC).)

Use Caution When Shopping for Debt

Avoid any debt relief organization – whether it is credit counseling, debt settlement, or any other service – that:
- Charges any fees before it settles your debts or enters you into a DMP plan
- Pressures you to make "voluntary contributions," which is really another name for fees
- Touts a "new government program" to bail out personal credit card debt
- Guarantees it can make your unsecured debt go away

- Tells you to stop communicating with your creditors, but does not explain the serious consequences
- Tells you it can stop all debt collection calls and lawsuits
- Guarantees that your unsecured debts can be paid off for pennies on the dollar
- Would not send you free information about the services it provides without requiring you to provide personal financial information, such as your credit card account numbers, and balances
- Tries to enroll you in a debt relief program without reviewing your financial situation with you
- Offers to enroll you in a DMP without teaching you budgeting and money management skills
- Demands that you make payments into a DMP before your creditors have accepted you into the program

Debt Consolidation

You may be able to lower your cost of credit by consolidating your debt through a second mortgage or a home equity line of credit. But, these loans require you to put up your home as collateral. If you cannot make the payments – or if your payments are late – you could lose your home.

What is more, consolidation loans have costs. In addition to interest, you may have to pay "points," with one point equal to one percent of the amount you borrow. Still, these loans may provide certain tax advantages that are not available with other kinds of credit.

Bankruptcy

Personal bankruptcy also may be an option, although its consequences are long-lasting and far-reaching. People who follow the bankruptcy rules receive a discharge – a court order that says they do not have to repay certain debts. However, bankruptcy information (both the date of the filing and the later date of discharge) stay on a credit report for 10 years and can make it difficult to get credit, buy a home, get life insurance, or sometimes get a job. Still, bankruptcy is a legal procedure that offers a fresh start for people who have gotten into financial difficulty and cannot satisfy their debts.

There are two main types of personal bankruptcy: Chapter 13 and Chapter 7. Each must be filed in federal bankruptcy court. Filing fees are several hundred dollars.

Chapter 13 allows people with a steady income to keep property, like a mortgaged house or a car, that they might otherwise lose through the bankruptcy process. In Chapter 13, the court approves a repayment plan that allows you to use your future income to pay off your debts during three to five years, rather than surrender any property. After you make all the payments under the plan, you receive a discharge of your debts.

Chapter 7 is known as "straight bankruptcy;" it involves liquidating all assets that are not exempt. Exempt property may include automobiles, work-related tools, and basic household furnishings. Some of your property may be sold by a court-appointed official, called a "trustee," or turned over to your creditors.

Both types of bankruptcy may get rid of unsecured debts and stop foreclosures, repossessions, garnishments and utility shut-offs, as well as debt collection activities. Both also provide exemptions that let you keep certain assets, although exemption amounts vary by state. Personal bankruptcy usually does not erase child support, alimony, fines, taxes, and some student loan obligations. And, unless you have an acceptable plan to catch up on your debt under Chapter 13, bankruptcy usually does not allow you to keep property when your creditor has an unpaid mortgage or security lien on it.

You must get credit counseling from a government-approved organization within six months before you file for any bankruptcy relief. You can find a state-by-state list of government-approved organizations at the U.S. Trustee Program, the organization within the U.S. Department of Justice (DOJ) that supervises bankruptcy cases and trustees. Also, before you file a Chapter 7 bankruptcy case, you must satisfy a "means test." This test requires you to confirm that your income does not exceed a certain amount. The amount varies by state and is publicized by the U.S. Trustee Program.

Debt Scams

Advance fee loans. Some companies guarantee you a loan if you pay them a fee in advance. The fee may range from $100 to several hundred dollars. Resist the temptation to follow up on these advance-fee loan guarantees. They may be illegal. It is true that many legitimate creditors offer extensions of credit through telemarketing and require an application or appraisal fee in advance. But, legitimate creditors never guarantee that you will get the loan – or even represent that a loan is likely. Under the FTC's Telemarketing Sales Rule, a seller or telemarketer who guarantees or represents a high likelihood of your getting a loan or some other extension of credit may not ask for – or accept – payment until you get the loan.

Credit repair. Be suspicious of claims from so-called "credit repair clinics." Many companies appeal to people with poor credit histories, promising to clean up their credit reports for a fee. But, anything these companies can do for you for a fee, you can do yourself – for free. You have the right to correct inaccurate information in your file, but no one – regardless of their claims – can remove accurate negative information from your credit report. Only time and a conscientious effort to repay your debts will improve your credit report. Federal – and some state – laws ban these companies from charging you a fee until the services are fully performed.

PART 6 | FINANCIAL APPS AND DATA SECURITY CONCERNS

CHAPTER 39

WHAT IS FINANCIAL TECHNOLOGY?

Financial technology, commonly known as "Fintech," is a broad term used to define any use of technology in businesses that provide financial services. Financial technology can be a software, service, or a company's product that provides digitally relevant financial services that are more efficient than traditional banking processes. Financial technology is a rapidly growing industry that primarily serves young adults and teenagers who are predominantly online. The popularity of financial technology lies in the fact that it brings present-day relevance to financial services along with precision and ease of use for younger consumers.

Financial technology digitizes money and helps monetize real-time consumer data for digital platforms. Several companies use technology such as artificial intelligence (AI) and blockchain in traditional financial services for safety, efficiency, and speed. As it is a booming sector, companies invest in different aspects of financial technology such as investments, saving plans, loan payments, stocks, and credit scores. Some popular financial technology companies include Stripe, Ripple, Chime, Coinbase, and Opendoor. These companies provide services ranging from real estate (Opendoor), mobile-only banking that facilitates no-fee checking accounts (Chime), secure cryptocurrency exchange (Coinbase), and international exchange (Ripple) to simple online payments (Stripe).

How Does Financial Technology Work?

Financial technology has been part of the economic sectors since the introduction of credit cards, ATMs, personal finance applications, and online trading. The latest technologies that work within financial technology include machine learning software and blockchain algorithms to simplify financial processes such as running credit risks and investing in hedge funds. It is unique to each service being provided and varies between different applications and adapts to automated customer services, chatbots, and artificial intelligence interfaces that also help reduce employment costs.

Types of Services

There are three categories to Fintech services that include:

- **Consumer-to-consumer (C2C).** A financial technology service that is involved in digital money transactions. These services allow consumers to interact with each other without mediators such as banks. They are used in money exchange applications such as Venmo. This kind of application is instantaneous, free of charge, and convenient.
- **Business-to-business (B2B).** These tools help integrated businesses function efficiently. Services such as cash management between businesses are the most prioritized in these tools. These services are beneficial for businesses as they provide liquidity, protection, and higher rates of return for businesses and their cash reserves.
- **Business-to-consumer (B2C).** Businesses that interact with customers, such as in the traditional banking sector or retail sector, make the most use of these services. PayPal is a clear example of B2C financial technology service. Such benefits of financial technology enable businesses to keep their customers satisfied by providing transparency in transactions.

Benefits of Financial Technology

- Greater security is guaranteed since Fintech employs data encryption and biometrics to secure consumer data. Many businesses are choosing to enlist financial technology for the monetary services they provide to assure consumers of security.
- Enhanced customer service and returns are the primary goals of financial institutions that use financial technology. These technologies provide better and digitally relevant services that help retain customers and thereby increase revenue.
- **Wider reach for businesses.** By integrating financial technology and mobile technology, companies can tap into a larger demographic since a significant section of the population belongs to the teenage and young adult age group that is continuously adapting to mobile and digital-based living.
- Convenience is a significant benefit of financial technology. It completely removes the need for mediators and lets the customer handle their finances directly along with improved connectivity. The ease with which finance services are obtained with financial technology instead of traditional methods is a bonus, especially for teenagers who wish to personally handle their finances.
- **Relevant payment approaches.** Recent advances in financial technology can ensure that businesses can provide invoices and collect money payments online with higher accuracy.

- **Better access to financial advice.** Individuals such as teenagers interested in managing their finances can avail the services of robo-advising for generalized topics. Many institutions utilize automated technology as the first point of contact for novice customers. With this approach, there is a lower risk of fraud or mismanagement as the algorithm employed is curated to provide accurate and real-time advice without the input of a human thereby also reducing errors.
- **Financial inclusivity.** Financial technology has led to ease of access to financial services previously reserved for a particular section of society, such as lending platforms, investment banking, and loan approvals. People across age groups and economic strata now have the opportunity to be financially literate.
- **Changing the insurance landscape.** Financial technology is bringing a change in traditional insurance provision by taking a majority of the procedures online such as online policy and data handling, and providing customized insurance policies.
- **Helping businesses manage cash more efficiently.** Financial technology services ranging from managing deposits for businesses to handling escrow (a legal concept where a neutral third party holds money for two parties during a business transaction) help simplify transactions, keep related documents secure and avoid outsourcing.

Technologies Involved in Financial Technology

Various technologies contribute to the efficiency of financial technology, such as:

- Blockchain is a system of recording valuable data which cannot be hacked or changed. It is highly preferred as it allows for secure storage of data and transaction records. All transactions with blockchain are encrypted, which reduces the risk of cyber-attacks. Blockchain is primarily used in managing cryptocurrencies.
- **Big data, data analytics.** Market and consumer data, though extensive, is valuable for financial technology companies. Collecting such data can help improve predictive analytics algorithms that can predict customer behavior about investments and other preferences.
- **Artificial intelligence (AI), machine learning (ML).** These technologies use algorithms to detect patterns in online processes and money transactions. These can also be used to detect fraudulent transactions, improve wealth management and credit scoring.
- Robotic process automation (RPA) involves robotics that can be used instead of human labor for repetitive actions in financial services. Robotics can be used for data collection, statistical analysis, communication through chatbots and automated e-mail systems, and managing transactions.

Applications and Uses of Fintech

Financial technology comes with various benefits and is slowly finding its way into all digital platforms that offer financial services. Financial technology is primarily used in fields such as:

- Banking
- Lending
- Mobile payments
- Trading
- Investments and savings
- Cryptocurrency
- Insurance
- Robo-advising
- Microfinance
- Crowdfunding platforms
- Online payments

Safety and Regulations in Financial Technology

Financial technology, though advantageous, has its share of risks. This drives the legal regulations that control the processes and how various corporations and governments use or misuse financial technology. It now comes with a set of regulatory technologies called "regtech" that helps companies address compliance and regulation policies.

Since financial technology finds applications in different industries, a comprehensive regulatory approach is necessary; combining existing and customized regulations that can help prevent threats of misuse and unnecessary exposure to hackers and misuse of data.

References

1. "Fintech," Built In, May 25, 2019.
2. "What Is Financial Technology or Fintech and Its Benefits?" Automeme, November 20, 2019.
3. Pack, Tyler. "Few Advantages of Financial Technology in the Retail Banking Industry," Fintech Weekly, February 28, 2020.
4. Walden, Stephanie. "What Is Fintech and How Does It Affect How I Bank?" Forbes Advisor, August 3, 2020.
5. Kagan, Julia. "Financial Technology – Fintech," Investopedia, August 28, 2020.
6. "Fintech (Financial Technology)," Corporate Finance Institute, January 31, 2020.
7. "Fintech Definition," Fintech Weekly, n.d.
8. "What Is Fintech – Financial Technology?" The American Deposit Management Company (ADM), September 29, 2020.
9. Kauflin, Jeff. "The 10 Biggest Fintech Companies in America 2020," *Forbes*, February 12, 2020.

CHAPTER 40

FINANCIAL ADVISORS AND APPS

About This Chapter: "Financial Advisors and Apps," © 2021 Omnigraphics.

Managing your assets, knowing where and when to invest for good returns, planning for retirement, or even planning your child's future education can sometimes be strenuous. Though one might have an idea on how to strategize and manage their assets, it would be much more beneficial to consult someone who is particularly skilled in the field of financial management.

Who Is a Financial Advisor?

A financial advisor is a professional who advises customers on financial matters based on their financial circumstances. The adviser consults with the clients on a variety of subjects including how much money the client should save, the types of accounts she/he should have, the types of insurance they should have, and even estate and tax planning.

In addition to being a financial advisor, the person also helps in educating the client on various financial options and trends available. Part of the advisor's job is to explain what is required in achieving the client's long-term objectives.

A few steps that can be followed to choose the right financial advisor are detailed below:

Financial Capability

Financial capability is knowing how to spend wisely, manage credit, and plan for the future. Financial capability is an effective way to help youth, no matter their circumstances, avoid common financial vulnerabilities and build economic stability.4 Youth should be educated about finances early in life and at pivotal points in their development and financial lives.

(Source: "Financial Capability & Literacy," Youth.gov.)

Deciding on Which Financial Part You Need Help With

It is better to decide which elements of your financial life require assistance before speaking with a financial advisor. Individuals with relatively simple financial lifestyles, such as young people without a family or major debt, may simply require assistance with the types of investments and planning for a better future.

People with more financial needs, on the other hand, may require further support. They may need assistance in attempting to establish college funds for their children, or navigate debt payment arrangements, and resolving tax issues.

Knowing the Types of Advisors

- Financial advisers that work on a fee-only (fiduciary) basis make money from fees the clients pay for their services. These costs might be calculated as a percentage of the assets a client manages, an hourly cost, or a fixed rate.
- Commission based on third-party sales is a source of income for certain types of financial advisors.
- There are companies that provide financial advice through certified financial planners (CFPs) with years of training and experience in various finance-related fields and are known as "registered investment advisors" (RIAs).
- Low-cost, computerized investing advice is provided by robo-advisors. These robo-advisors focus on helping customers invest for mid- and long-term goals, such as retirement, using prebuilt diversified exchange-traded fund (ETF) portfolios.

Role of Technology in Financial Advising

Professional financial planning has been substantially influenced by technological advancements. Independent advisors, registered representatives, and even accountants have come to rely on sophisticated financial tools to assist them, by not just creating proper investment and retirement plans for their customers, but also to better engage them.

The top financial planning software used by professionals are mentioned below:

MoneyGuidePro®. It is a visually engaging, user-friendly software program developed by PIEtech® in 2001. The primary interface is meant to completely engage the customer, featuring a play zone where one may experiment with various alternatives to see how they could affect the result. The adviser, on the other hand, retains complete control over the software, including which sections of it the client is permitted to view. MoneyGuidePro® also has numerous interactive interfaces with third-party products.

eMoney Advisor. The eMoney software is noted for its comprehensive cash flow analysis module and delivers a very in-depth application. One of eMoney's top features is its financial feed, which offers real-time data, alerts, and news to advisers, allowing them to be on top of crucial client and market circumstances. The eMoney client portal is another significant feature that allows clients to print a copy of their accounts at any time.

MoneyTree. Its core capabilities provide considerable flexibility that focuses on a variety of goals, such as retirement, estate planning, or education finance plans.

NaviPlan®. It is most popular among dual registered advisors since it is easily expandable to a variety of client numbers. It covers a full examination of assets and liabilities, including debt, as well as a retirement study of accumulations and disbursements.

Uses of Financial Advisors and Software

Though the services offered by financial advisors may vary from person to person, they all tend to provide information and help in the following:

- Investment advice
- Debt management
- Budgeting
- Insurance coverage and options
- Tax planning
- Retirement planning
- Estate planning
- Educational planning

Financial advisors may also provide emotional support and perspective during difficult economic times, in addition to investment management and financial planning. Client demand for financial advisors soared significantly during the start of the *Coronavirus* pandemic in March 2020.

References

1. Fontinelle, Amy. "What Do Financial Advisors Do?" Investopedia, January 25, 2021.
2. "How to Choose a Financial Advisor," *Forbes*, August 11, 2020.
3. Maverick, J.B. "Top 5 Software Programs Used by Financial Advisors," Investopedia, October 12, 2019.

CHAPTER 41
BUDGETING APPS

About This Chapter: "Budgeting Apps," © 2021 Omnigraphics.

Money management is a skill with some people being more mathematically or systematically inclined than others. Though classrooms educate youngsters with ideas of money, parents should presumably reinforce the lessons at home; since, financial literacy and its practical applications are lifetime pursuits.

While the notion of budgeting has been around for decades, it has taken on a completely new appearance and feel in recent years due to advances in technology. Companies are striving to fill a new business area known as "FinTech" (financial technology) by giving digital answers to common financial concerns, such as budgeting, saving, investing, life insurance, and much more.

Rise of Technology in Financial Management

Teenagers and young adults who grow up with technology have an edge when it comes to becoming financially aware and self-sufficient. Smartphones, which are always within reach, may serve as additional tutors and enforcers of financial management.

The following are a few money management, financial literacy, and budgeting applications:

Tracking Your Money and Expenses

Some banks and credit unions provide online financial management tools including income and spending tracking budget, and cash flow tools. If you have an account at a bank or credit union, check to see if these tools may be available for you.

You may also want to explore using online financial management tools. When you enter personal or banking information ensure the website is secure.

(Source: "A Financial Empowerment Toolkit for Community Volunteers," Consumer Financial Protection Bureau (CFPB).)

Financial Literacy Apps for Teens

- **Toshl Finance.** This checkbook ledger for the digital era assists young adults in creating monthly budgets and tracking expenditures. The user can keep track of her or his expenses and categorize them accordingly.
- **Left to Spend.** This app is a budgeting app at the most basic level. While the app is not as sophisticated as some of the others on this list, it stands out for its simplicity. Users can set a spending limit and deduct their expenses with regular use.
- **Mint.** It is a popular software used by many financial advisors and corporations alike. Mint connects all your personal accounts, loans, and credit cards, providing instant access and tracking.

Budgeting Simulation Apps for Teens

- **SmartyPig.** This progress-tracking software is perfect for preteens and teenagers who are starting to learn how to apply financial literacy in real-life situations. The software allows users to set financial objectives and then update them as milestones when accomplished.
- **P2K Money.** It extends the lesson by documenting and monitoring allowances, same as the ideas presented in Savings Spree. One of the app's built-in features allows users to earn extra money by doing domestic tasks.
- **iAllowance.** It is a money-tracking software same as SmartyPig and P2K Money. The software provides a forum for parents/guardians and teenagers to collaborate on money management practices and other apps.

Uses of a Budgeting App

Real-Time Information

Budgeting applications gather data from all your different accounts and display it on a single dashboard. With just one click, you can launch the app and see real-time balances for all your bank, investment, and credit card accounts.

Automatic Alerts

Automatic notifications notify you of significant occurrences even if you do not access the app. For example, if a large, unexpected transaction occurs in one of your accounts, an app can notify you, providing you the opportunity to investigate for fraud. Apps may also alert you on upcoming bill due dates, allowing you to prevent missing or late payments, which can negatively impact your credit score.

Tracking Progress

Many budgeting applications will track expenses over time, allowing you to track both your general financial success and your progress toward goals. Most applications allow customers to create savings objectives. For instance, you may set aside $500 for a weekend getaway. In the app, you may set a goal, choose a savings account, and keep track of your progress. The app will monitor your progress towards your goal each time you make a deposit to your savings account. This ensures that you can see how close you are to that happy weekend.

If you are not sure where your money goes, it is usually because you are not sticking to a budget plan. It is important to have a budget to keep track of your finances. You can make required modifications and better manage your finances once you know where and how much money you are spending.

References

1. Sheppard, Rebecca. "10 Personal Finance Apps for Teens and Young Adults," Yahoo Finance, July 31, 2015.
2. Compton Game, Shannah. "Should You Use Budgeting Apps to Manage Your Money?" Policy Genius, November 24, 2015.
3. Porter, TJ. "5 Reasons to Use a Budgeting App to Manage Your Finances," Money Crashers, November 18, 2020.
4. Pal, Anangh. "Budgeting Apps: How Are They Beneficial?" Outlook Money, December 24, 2020.

CHAPTER 42
CHECKBOOK LEDGER APPS

Back in the day, to keep track of their balances, people adopted paper check ledgers to record withdrawals and deposits to their bank accounts. Account holders totaled up goods with a pen and notepad to keep a running balance of available cash.

According to the American Bankers Association (ABA), more than two-thirds of bank clients now perform their banking online or through a mobile app. Many customers prefer to check balances and keep their records online, enabling banks to do the job for them. While this approach is quite user-friendly, there are situations when keeping a check ledger is necessary. The following are a few applications that can be used as a checkbook ledger:

- **Mint.** The Mint application by Intuit Inc. has a user rating of 4.5 out of 5, with more than 10 million users. This free app manages personal finances by double-entry bookkeeping method and is available on Android and iOS devices. A unique feature of this app is that it can generate spending reports daily.
- **Volkron CheckBook.** This checkbook by Volkron Development has more than 100,000 users and an excellent user rating. This free application that can be found on the Google Play Store, offers users a 14-day free trial period of their premium version. A few of the key features are as follows:
  - It supports different number formats and currencies.
  - It allows the creation of duplicate transactions.
  - It has a backup and restore to Dropbox option.
- **Free Checkbook Ledger.** Teelu Apps developed this ledger app, which is same as the Volkron app. It has more than 100,000 downloads. This app can be downloaded from the Google Play Store. The main features of the app are as follows:
  - Scheduled or recurring transactions

    - Options to exports transactions
    - Unlimited accounts
    - Backup options
- **Checkbook - Account Tracker.** This app, which is developed by Polycents, has a 4.1 out of 5 user rating and is available for both Android and iOS devices. This user-friendly app is used by more than 100,000 people and has an option to export the ledger from other applications or backup.
- **Checkbook Plus.** This app is developed by BlacKCat Software Solutions and is used to manage one's everyday transactions. Users who opt for the premium version can enjoy an ad-free experience.

A few other highly rated apps are:
- Debt Book
- EZ Register
- Fudget
- Simplifi
- GnuCash
- Goodbudget
- Prism Pay Bills
- Quicken
- ChartBills
- NerdWallet

Most of the apps have basic features and functions, such as:
- Setting up options to pay utility bills
- Calendar option to keep track of the spending
- Monthly saving options
- Uploading photos of bills and receipts
- Trading options
- Retirement savings plans
- Syncing of multiple accounts
- Frequent updates and notifications

The apps that are mentioned here are some of the highest user-rated apps, which are all free to use. However, individuals wishing to utilize exclusive features and options will need to upgrade to a premium version of these apps by paying a certain amount either monthly or as a one-time option, depending on the application.

References

1. Bernazzani, Sophia. "A Beginner's Guide to General Ledgers," HubSpot, July 25, 2019.
2. Oneil, Erin. "4 Reasons to Keep a Physical Check Ledger," The Balance, May 25, 2021.
3. "Best 10 Apps to Balance Checkbook," App Grooves, December 5, 2020.
4. "5 Best Apps for Balancing Your Checkbook," Current Blog, November 28, 2020.
5. "App Data Solutions to Accelerate Ecosystem Success," Search Man, n.d.

CHAPTER 43
APPS TO PAY BILLS

About This Chapter: "Apps to Pay Bills," © 2021 Omnigraphics.

Paying your bills and completing other regular payments have become simpler, safer, and more secure with the help of financial technology. Online payment and payment apps help you pay bills at your home's comfort. All that is required is a reliable data connection and your financial details at hand. The payment apps keep things virtual, quick, and ensure maximum security. Before understanding the types of apps available for bill payments, it may be helpful to learn the basics of these apps and how they function.

Mobile payment and wallet apps are some of the most popular types of payment methods used to pay bills online. A mobile payment is a financial transaction made on a portable electronic device. Banks use financial technology to help their customers make instant payments and send money digitally from their accounts. These mobile payment apps are also used in stores to make onsite payments, and the amount is deducted from the customer's bank or store account. The payment details are encrypted, which makes such payments more secure and efficient.

A mobile wallet is a digital wallet that simplifies banking transactions and other online payments by storing card information on mobile devices. These apps are convenient for store purchases that are registered with the payment app. These apps store card information by assigning a personal identification format such as a QR code. During a transaction, the app uses near field communication (NFC) and the personal identification format to send the user's payment information to the business' point of sale terminal. Mobile wallets offer security and encryption for customers and faster payments for businesses.

Many mobile payment apps are available for paying regular bills and keeping track of other payments. Some of them include:

- **PayPal.** It is one of the first payment apps to provide online payments and digital wallet services, beginning with eBay transactions. It is now used to transfer money between U.S.-based and foreign accounts. Payments from credit cards and currency conversions are charged on the app. The app is user-friendly and offers security. The users and merchants are charged for using the app.

- **Venmo.** A subsidiary of PayPal, the app (available in Google Play and App Store) is primarily used to send and receive money. It has nearly 60 million users and does not charge users for sending money from their linked debit card account. Those using a credit card to use the app are charged a 3-percent fee. It is also an accepted mode of payment among many businesses.
- **Cash App.** It functions as a mobile credit card processor and allows users to send and receive money from anyone with a Cash App account. The transaction is free of charge and is drawn from a linked debit card. It offers users a digital wallet, and its unique feature is that it allows users to buy and sell Bitcoin (a type of cryptocurrency) as well. This app has a transfer limit and transactions are chargeable if using a credit card.
- **Zelle.** It is a popular banking app offered by some major banking institutions in the United States that provides same-day money transfers. The app allows users to use its financial services either from a smartphone or a laptop. Zelle does not charge its users for any transactions. The use of this app does not require a download or an installation. Zelle allows transactions solely from a primary account and requires the sender and receiver to have accounts with participating banks for successful transactions.
- **Google Pay.** It requires the user to have a Gmail account and does not charge for any money transactions between contacts. The app may take upto 24 hours for the transferred funds to reflect on both accounts. It is a relatively simple app to use and is well integrated into other Google services.
- **Facebook Messenger.** It allows users and online businesses to send and receive payments. Users need to have a Facebook account and a linked debit card. Payment information is kept private, and the app has a simple user interface. The payments may take five working days to reflect in the account.
- **Wise.** It is predominantly used for international money transfers and is a cheaper option as it charges a standard exchange rate instead of bank rates. Wise is available to install on Android and iOS devices and secure encryption that protects sensitive bank information. Wise allows users to transfer up to $15,000 per day with a debit card and $2,000 in a day, and $8,000 every week within permitted states in the United States and specific countries outside of the United States.
- **Stripe.** It provides support for invoices and regular billing for small businesses and freelancers. It is a simple app and lets users seamlessly

transfer information to other payment apps. Stripe accepts payments through all major credit and debit card providers in various countries. Stripe has payment card industry (PCI) service provider level 1 certification and provides instant payouts.

- **QuickBooks Online Mobile.** It is an excellent app for small businesses. It helps keep track of tax payments, provides business estimates, connects bookkeeping, manages cash and bills, catalogs cash deductions and business expenses, and invoices. It can set reminders for regular payments and also provides online payment service. QuickBooks uses RSA encryption, secure sockets layer (SSL), and digital certificates for security. With this app, it is also easier to cancel a wrong transaction.

Most payment apps use a mobile wallet and a mobile payment method. It is also important to ensure that the devices these apps work on are protected from any form of cybercrime. Though the apps come with their own encryption and other security features, there are ways to protect our devices, and with them, our sensitive information such as payment and account information which are susceptible to fraud. Some points to remember are:

- Use the smartphone or mobile device as privately as possible.
- Use social networking apps with caution.
- Do not use any payment apps on an unsecured Wi-Fi network.
- Install security software on the device.
- Check the account attached to the payment apps regularly for any fraudulent activity.
- Do not leave the device unattended and unlocked.
- Maintain unique passwords for the device and app for an added layer of security.

Financial institutions are promoting their online services more and more. Some financial institutions even offer reductions in fees if you do all your banking online and never enter a physical branch. Online services have developed to the point where you can do pretty much anything a teller can, if not more.

Key services include:

- At-a-glance account information
- Account alerts
- Access to prior statements
- Transaction search
- Automatic savings plan
- Money transfers
- E-bills and bill pay

(Source: "Online and Mobile Banking," MyCreditUnion.gov.)

- Keep a note of your device's details, such as the model number, serial number, and IMEI number, in case you need to file a report with the police.

In case the device or smartphone is stolen, there are ways one can go about it, such as:

- Trying to call the smartphone to locate it
- Using the security software to erase the information stored on the device
- Changing all passwords immediately and contacting the banks or app helplines for further procedures
- Reporting the theft

References

1. Grant, Mitchell. "Mobile Payment," Investopedia, April 21, 2021.
2. Kenton, Will. "Mobile Wallet Definition," Investopedia, August 27, 2020.
3. Brock, Melissa. "Best Payment Apps," Investopedia, May 2, 2021.
4. Rosenberg, Eric. "Best Payment Apps," The Balance, March 23, 2021.
5. "Mobile Wallet Services Protection," Federal Communications Commission (FCC), February 25, 2020.

CHAPTER 44
INVESTMENT AND MONEY TRACKING APPS

About This Chapter: "Investment and Money Tracking Apps," © 2021 Omnigraphics.

Investments intend to set aside money in the hope of receiving a good benefit or return in the future. In other words, to invest is to hold an asset or an item with the intention of earning money from it or benefiting from its appreciation.

Any mix of financial assets, such as stocks, bonds, mutual funds, exchange-traded funds (ETFs), and individual retirement accounts (IRAs) are considered as investments. Rent, utilities, equipment, furnishings, inventory, permits, insurance, marketing, and employees are just a few of the examples of an investment for a small size company. Keeping track of all these assets can be difficult. To stay on budget, it is critical to maintain all your assets and know what is going on with them on a regular basis.

Tracking Investments

A decade ago, Microsoft Money (personal finance software) was one of the best options for the average investor who wanted to keep track of their money. It enabled individuals to keep track of their stock, bonds, mutual funds, real estate, cash equivalents, and certificates of deposit portfolios. It managed dividend reinvestment schemes, computed tax bases, and provided up-to-date information by pulling real-time changes from online stock prices.

Several other software packages were developed over the years with some of them being hosted online as a service paradigm, while others are apps that can be installed on your computers or phones.

Applications for Investment and Money Management

A few popular applications to keep track of your assets and investments are:

- **Personal Capital.** It keeps track of and categorizes a person's credit and debit card purchases. The software generates graphs that show your monthly cash inflow as well as your monthly spending. The free financial dashboard and the wealth management service are the two available versions. The wealth management option offers an investment management service that functions similarly to a Robo advisor but with live help. Budgeting and a cash flow analyzer are included in the free financial dashboard. The software may also assist you with retirement planning and give an investing checkup.

- **Expensify.** It is a user-friendly app for creating expenditure reports on the go and is available for Android and iOS devices. Expensify allows you to take images of receipts and manually track costs, making it a must-have for regular business travels. When you click a picture of a receipt using the Expensify app, the software interprets it and converts it into an expense. You may categorize your spending by kinds, such as mileage, travel, and meals. Expensify is free for individuals and costs only $5 per month for team usage.
- **SigFig Wealth Management.** SigFig consolidates your investment accounts from more than 50 prominent brokerages into a single dashboard, giving you a real-time picture of every stock, mutual fund, ETF, and option you hold. Weekly e-mail summaries of account performance, news that affects your portfolio, and notifications on your top gainers and losers will be sent to you. The software examines your portfolio automatically to uncover hidden costs and overexposure to a particular stock or industry. With rebalancing, dividend reinvestment, and tax-efficient tactics, SigFig will optimize your portfolio and give regular monitoring to keep it on track.
- **Yahoo Finance.** This app provides a user-friendly interface that allows you to keep track of your stocks, commodities, bonds, and currencies. Customized news and notifications, as well as real-time market updates, are also available on the app.
- **Morningstar's Portfolio Manager.** The Morningstar Investment Management LLC's Portfolio Manager app requires you to manually enter details of each of your investments. The app gives you basic information on all your assets, such as their current price, daily value fluctuations, and percent weight in your entire portfolio. It also gives detailed information on the overall performance of a portfolio and analyses the overall return of your portfolio by month and year. The app can be downloaded for free from the Apple App Store and Google Play Store. Users can upgrade to a premium version at a certain rate with a 14-day free trial period.
- **Wally.** It is a vibrant program with a friendly interface and several useful expense-tracking features. This app can be downloaded for free from the

Apple App Store and Google Play Store. Wally, like other expense-tracking applications, allows you to capture images of receipts or manually input costs and classify them. It also keeps track of your earnings and forecasts your monthly savings. The app is more suitable for people who own micro-businesses or side businesses.

- **Fresh Books.** It is a comprehensive alternative for entrepreneurs who want a complete accounting program that also offers mobile expense-tracking capabilities. It can be downloaded by both iOS and Android users on their devices. This cloud-based accounting program starts at $9.95 per month for a single user and five clients and has $29.95 monthly plan, which includes an unlimited number of clients, an extra staff member, and project management tools.
- **Mint.** It is one of the most popular spending tracker applications for personal finance. This software is completely free and works with a variety of banks and lenders. It is developed by Intuit, one of the leading financial software companies. Expense tracking, bills, and credit monitoring, and budgeting are all made easier with this app.
- **Mvelopes.** This easy-to-use software is a budgeting app with a unique feature that suggests a spending strategy. The app offers different categories to track expenditure, wherein the user can set a limit for the amount that has to be spent on each category. Exceeding that limit will allow the app to notify the user. This app is available on both Apple App Store and Google Play Store.

Uses of Money Tracking Apps

Portfolio management applications allow you to keep track of your money from anywhere at any time. Some programs integrate with your current accounts, while others need you to manually enter data about your investments. The apps and latest software not only help individuals and companies to keep track of their expenses but also to give insight and offer better spending solutions for their investments. The most important features offered by the apps for businesses are:

- Capture and organizing receipts
- Organizing tax deductions
- Tracking sales
- Running reports
- Managing contractors and vendors
- Providing secure access
- Tracking inventories and projects
- Automating workflows
- Offering insight and analytics

References

1. "Top 10 Expense Tracker," Business News Daily, May 16, 2020.
2. Kennon, Joshua. "The Easiest Ways to Track Investments," The Balance, February 10, 2021.
3. Folger, Jean. "4 Top Portfolio Management Apps," Investopedia, January 2, 2020.
4. "5 Best Investment Apps for Managing Your Portfolio," *Forbes*, April 12, 2021.

CHAPTER 45

IDENTITY THEFT AND IDENTITY FRAUD

About This Chapter: Text beginning with the heading "What Is Identity Theft?" is excerpted from "What to Know about Identity Theft," Federal Trade Commission (FTC), March 2021; Text under the heading "New Protections Available for Minors under 16" is excerpted from "New Protections Available for Minors under 16," Federal Trade Commission (FTC), March 11, 2019.

What Is Identity Theft?

Identity theft is when someone uses your personal or financial information without your permission.

They might steal your name and address, credit card, or bank account numbers, Social Security number, or medical insurance account numbers. And they could use them to:

- Buy things with your credit cards.
- Get new credit cards in your name.
- Open a phone, electricity, or gas account in your name.
- Steal your tax refund.
- Use your health insurance to get medical care.
- Pretend to be you if they are arrested.

How to Protect Yourself against Identity Theft

Taking steps to protect your personal information can help you avoid identity theft. Here is what you can do to stay ahead of identity thieves.

What Do Thieves Do with Your Information?

Once identity thieves have your personal information, they can drain your bank account, run up charges on your credit cards, open new utility accounts, or get medical treatment on your health insurance. An identity thief can file a tax refund in your name and get your refund. In some extreme cases, a thief might even give your name to the police during an arrest.

(Source: "Warning Signs of Identity Theft," IdentityTheft.gov, Federal Trade Commission (FTC).)

Protect Documents That Have Personal Information

Keep your financial records, Social Security and Medicare cards, and any other documents that have personal information in a safe place. When you decide to get rid of those documents, shred them before you throw them away. If you do not have a shredder, look for a local shred day, or use a marker to block out account numbers.

If you get statements with personal information in the mail, take your mail out of the mailbox as soon as you can.

Ask Questions before Giving Out Your Social Security Number

Some organizations need your Social Security number to identify you. Those organizations include the IRS, your bank, and your employer. Organizations like these that do need your Social Security number will not call, e-mail, or text you to ask for it.

Other organizations that might ask you for your Social Security number might not really need it. Those organizations include a medical provider, a company, or your child's school. Ask these questions before you give them your Social Security number:

- Why do you need it?
- How will you protect it?
- Can you use a different identifier?
- Can you use just the last four digits of my Social Security number?

Protect Your Information from Scammers Online and on Your Phone

If you are logging in to an online account, use a strong password.

Add multifactor authentication for accounts that offer it. Multifactor authentication offers extra security by requiring two or more credentials to log in to your account. The additional credentials you need to log in to your account fall into two categories: something you have – such as a passcode you get via text message or an authentication app, or something you are – such as a scan of your fingerprint, your retina, or your face. Multifactor authentication makes it harder for scammers to log in to your accounts if they do get your username and password.

Do not give your personal information to someone who calls, e-mails, or texts you. It could be a scammer trying to steal your information.

How to Know If Someone Stole Your Identity

In addition to taking steps to protect your information, it pays to know how to tell if someone stole your identity. There are things you can do yourself to detect identity theft. There also are companies that sell credit and identity monitoring services.

What You Can Do to Detect Identity Theft

Here is what you can do to spot identity theft:

- **Track what bills you owe and when they are due.** If you stop getting a bill, that could be a sign that someone changed your billing address.

If you discover that someone is misusing your personal information, visit IdentityTheft.gov to report and recover from identity theft.

- **Review your bills.** Charges for things you did not buy could be a sign of identity theft. So could a new bill you did not expect.
- **Check your bank account statement.** Withdrawals you did not make could be a sign of identity theft.
- **Get and review your credit reports.** Accounts in your name that you do not recognize could be a sign of identity theft.

Monitoring Services, Recovery Services, and Identity Theft Insurance

Many companies sell identity theft protection services that may include credit monitoring, identity monitoring, identity recovery services, and identity theft insurance. These services also might be offered by your:

- Bank or credit union
- Credit card provider
- Employer's benefits program
- Insurance company

Credit Monitoring Services

Credit monitoring services scan activity that shows up on your credit reports. They might monitor activity at one, two, or all three of the major credit bureaus – Equifax, Experian, and TransUnion.

Credit monitoring services will usually alert you when:

- A company checks your credit history
- A new loan or credit card account appears on your credit reports
- A creditor or debt collector says your payment is late
- Public records show that you filed for bankruptcy
- Someone files a lawsuit against you
- Your credit limit changes
- Your personal information, such as your name, address, or phone number, changes

Credit monitoring services will not alert you when:

- Someone withdraws money from your bank account
- Someone uses your Social Security number to file a tax return and collect your refund

If you are considering using a credit monitoring service, here are some questions you can ask them:

- How often do you check credit reports for changes?
- Which of the three credit bureaus do you monitor?
- Is there a limit to how often I can review my credit reports?
- Will I be charged each time I review my credit reports?
- Are other services included, such as access to my credit score?

Identity Monitoring Services

Companies that offer identity monitoring services check databases that collect different types of information to see if they contain new or inaccurate information about you. Those could be a sign that someone is using your personal information. These services can detect uses of your personal information that will not show up on your credit report.

Identity monitoring services may tell you when your information shows up in:

- A change of address request
- Court or arrest records
- Orders for new utility, cable, or wireless services
- An application for a payday loan
- A request to cash a check
- On social media
- On websites that identity thieves use to trade stolen information

Most identity monitoring services will not alert if someone uses your information to:

- File a tax return and collect your refund
- Get Medicare benefits
- Get Medicaid benefits
- Get welfare benefits
- Claim Social Security benefits
- Claim unemployment benefits

Identity Recovery Services

Companies that sell credit and identity monitoring services also may offer identity recovery services to help you fix any damage caused by identity theft. These services may be included or cost extra. Some of the services they offer may be things you can do on your own for little or no cost.

Identity recovery services typically give you access to counselors or case managers who will help you recover your identity. They may:

- Help you write letters to creditors and debt collectors
- Place a freeze on your credit report to prevent an identity thief from opening new accounts in your name
- Guide you through documents you have to review

Some services will represent you in dealing with creditors or other institutions if you formally grant them authority to act on your behalf.

Identity Theft Insurance

Companies that sell monitoring services also may offer identity theft insurance. These services may be included or cost extra.

Identity theft insurance may cover:

- Out-of-pocket expenses directly associated with reclaiming your identity, such as:
  - The cost of copying documents
  - Postage costs for sending documents
  - Costs for getting documents notarized
- Wages you lost
- Legal fees you paid

Identity theft insurance generally will not reimburse you for money stolen or financial loss resulting from the theft. Most policies will not pay if your loss is covered by your homeowner's or renter's insurance. If you are considering getting identity theft insurance, ask about the deductible and find out what is covered and what is not.

New Protections Available for Minors under 16

Young people now have more protection from identity theft and fraud, thanks to a new federal law that went into effect September 21st, 2018. The new law lets parents and child welfare representatives of people under 16, as well as legal guardians, request a security freeze, also called a "credit freeze," on their behalf. Taking this step can help protect a young person from identity theft and fraud – and it is free.

Identity theft happens when someone misuses your personal information, such as a Social Security number, to open accounts, file taxes, or make purchases. Hackers, thieves, and even people you know might steal your identity. Minors typically do not have credit reports, which means that a young person may not find out about issues with their credit reports until they first try to get credit – perhaps even years later.

While a security freeze will not affect anything already on your credit report, it restricts access to your report. That makes it harder for identity thieves to open new accounts using your personal information. With the new law, it is free to freeze and unfreeze your credit file at the three nationwide consumer reporting agencies – Equifax, Experian, and TransUnion. To find contact information for placing a free credit freeze, visit IdentityTheft.gov/credit bureau contacts.

The new law also lets people like parents, guardians, and representatives acting on behalf of a young person in foster care proactively protect a young person's credit file by freezing it.

If the nationwide credit reporting agencies do not have a file on the child, they will create one so they can freeze it. This record cannot be used for credit purposes. It is there just to make sure the child's record is frozen and protected against identity theft and fraud.

Depending on the adult's relationship to the child, there are different procedures to put a freeze in place. Parents need to show proof of their authority, such as a birth certificate, to freeze or unfreeze the credit file for their child under 16. The new law says that child welfare or probation agency representatives acting on behalf of a young person in foster care can request a security freeze for that child. They have to show documentation certifying that the child is in the agency's care, such as a written communication or an official letter from the child welfare or probation agency or its designee. Child welfare agencies who already work with consumer reporting agencies to pull and review credit reports for youth in their care can use the same company contacts and liaisons to facilitate the security freeze process.

CHAPTER 46
DATA SECURITY

About This Chapter: "Data Security," © 2021 Omnigraphics.

Data security is the process of securing digital information from illegal access, corruption, or theft. It comprises all aspects of information security, from the physical safety of hardware and storage devices to administrative and access controls, as well as the security of software applications.

Many teenagers and young adults today have smartphones, laptops, and access to unlimited information from the Internet and are technologically more knowledgeable than most adults. While many assume that adolescents use their gadgets only for video games and social networking, today the fact is that many teenagers utilize technology for both entertainment and knowledge.

Online Danger for Kids and Adolescents

Malware Content

To obtain personal information, cyber thieves frequently employ malware. Malware is any harmful application or code that causes system damage.

Hackers today know how to get users to download such malware and innocent children usually fall for the trap.

Online Scams

- **Fake membership.** Youngsters tend to like being in groups or clubs, and certain fake membership schemes may trick them and make them sign up and pay money.
- **Online contests.** Certain youngsters love to take part in contests, such as beauty contests, online games, cooking, and music contests. They might be scams to collect information or identity theft.
- **Popups.** Online popup notifications to update your software might be harmful, as they may contain viruses. It is safer not to download any unknown online updates.

- Torrents are commonly used to download movies and songs. Teens using this to download content from the Internet should be cautious as to what they are downloading to their devices.

Online Shopping and Scams

It is not a shock that more than 50 percent of Internet users buy products and shop online nowadays. The Internet offers tons of shopping and e-cart websites to choose from millions of products. Teenagers must be aware of the sites they use and should only opt to shop from reputed websites. Fake sites and scams tend to extract money, use your personal details, card details, locations, and even hack into personal devices.

Social Media

Social media has drastically changed the lives of young people online. While it helps teenagers to maintain relationships with family and friends, even over long distances, they also have a lot of life's hazards online. Social media is meant to persuade people to be part of a community. And although they work as virtual communities, you may easily overlook how many individuals are able to engage with friends online. Many young people share essential information on social media without understanding the consequences and are prone to identity robbery and other illegal activities.

Predators and Stalkers

Predators – people who seek to create an inadequate connection or to encourage them to conduct themselves inadequately – are a greater issue in Internet safety. Many of the most popular social media websites and applications have chat rooms and other places where individuals may communicate more with people they do not know. Parents should warn adolescents that even an innocent photo may disclose information about their age, schools where they arc going, and even personal details.

Data Security Applications

Recent data breaches and cyberattacks raise the question of consumer protection against harmful hackers or cybercriminals. Financial technology, often known as "FinTech," helps in maintaining financial safety.

A few reliable apps to protect financial data are:

- **Mint.** The Mint app by Inuit helps to manage all financial aspects at a single point of contact. The app is customized with Verisign and uses multi-factor authentication.
- **Lifelock App.** The Lifelock app by Norton can be used for both personal computers and mobile phones. It functions on a 360-degree concept that helps to:
  - Protect data and identity from device hacking and cyberattacks
  - Resolve any identity theft issues

Taking Care of Your Information

Just as you have to protect you money, you also have to protect your personal information. Never give out personal information, such as account numbers, passwords, or answers to security questions over the phone or through e-mail. Banks, credit unions, and other financial institutions will never call or e-mail you asking you to verify personal information.

(Source: "A Financial Empowerment Toolkit for Community Volunteers," Consumer Financial Protection Bureau (CFPB).)

    - Monitors any threat to identity and data
- **Identity Guard.** Aura industries has developed this app that focuses on machine learning and artificial intelligence to protect your personal and financial data.

Steps to Protect Data

It is important to note that no service provider or application will substitute proper safety measures when selecting an app or service provider. Some of the safest ways to secure your financial information against financial violations and cyber threats are:

- Never access bank accounts or member accounts using public devices.
- Use a virtual private network (VPN) at home and on your personal device. You can utilize VPN services that simply demand the press of a button before using the Internet actively.
- Shred papers and documents that include confidential information.
- Always shop on reputable websites. Avoid shopping from unknown vendors who could be scamming you.
- Do not give your Social Security number (SSN), birth date, or bank account number for personal identity information to anyone over the phone. In general, these data will not be requested by your financial service providers by phone.
- Never transfer money online to unknown persons, especially those that randomly approach you by phone, message, or e-mail.

References

1. "What Is Data Security?" IBM, May 12, 2020.
2. Chester, Dean. "Internet Safety for Teens, Kids, and Students," Cool Tech Zone, July 3, 2021.
3. "Best Apps for Protecting Your Financial Data," SeaCoast Bank, December 23, 2019.
4. "Online Teen Safety Guide," StaySafe.org, October 18, 2017.

PART 7 | IF YOU NEED MORE HELP OR INFORMATION

CHAPTER 47
RESOURCES FOR FINANCIAL INFORMATION

About This Chapter: Resources in this chapter were compiled from several sources deemed reliable; all contact information was verified and updated in July 2021.

Budgeting and Financial Information

American Bankers Association (ABA)

1120 Connecticut Ave., N.W.
Washington, DC 20036
Toll-Free: 800-BANKERS (800-226-5377)
Website: www.aba.com
E-mail: support@aba.com

American Financial Services Association (AFSA) Education Foundation

919 18th St., N.W., Ste. 300
Washington, DC 20006-5517
Toll-Free: 888-400-7577
Website: www.afsaef.org
E-mail: info@afsaef.org

American Institute of Certified Public Accountants (AICPA)

220 Leigh Farm Rd.
Durham, NC 27707-8110
Toll-Free: 888-777-7077
Phone: 919-402-4500
Fax: 919-402-4505
Website: www.aicpa.org
E-mail: service@aicpa.org

Asset Builders of America
1213 N. Sherman Ave., Ste. 195
Madison, WI 53704
Phone: 608-663-6332
Website: www.assetbuilders.org
E-mail: info@assetbuilders.org

Bloomberg Finance L.P.
731 Lexington Ave.
New York, NY 10022
Phone: 212-318-2000
Website: www.bloomberg.com

Certified Financial Planner Board of Standards, Inc.
1425 K St., N.W., Ste. 800
Washington, DC 20005
Toll-Free: 800-487-1497
Phone: 202-379-2200
Fax: 202-379-2299
Website: www.cfp.net
E-mail: mail@cfpboard.org

Council for Economic Education (CEE)
122 E. 42nd St., Ste. 1012
New York, NY 10168
Phone: 212-827-3600
Fax: 212-827-3610
Website: councilforeconed.org
E-mail: info@councilforeconed.org

Employee Benefit Research Institute (EBRI)
901 D St., S.W., Ste. 802
Washington, DC 20024
Phone: 202-659-0670
Fax: 202-775-6360
Website: www.ebri.org
E-mail: info@ebri.org

Federal Deposit Insurance Corporation (FDIC)

1310 Courthouse Rd.
Arlington, VA 22201
Toll-Free: 877-ASK-FDIC (877-275-3342)
Toll-Free TDD: 800-925-4618
Website: www.fdic.gov

Federal Trade Commission (FTC)

600 Pennsylvania Ave., N.W.
Washington, DC 20580
Phone: 202-326-2222
Website: www.ftc.gov

Financial Planning Association (FPA)

1290 Bdwy., Ste. 1625
Denver, CO 80203
Toll-Free: 800-322-4237
Phone: 303-759-4900
Fax: 303-759-0749
Website: www.onefpa.org
E-mail: info@onefpa.org

InCharge Education Foundation

5750 Major Blvd., Ste. 300
Orlando, FL 32819
Toll-Free: 866-721-3925
Website: www.incharge.org/foundation

Institute for Financial Literacy (IFL)

P.O. Box 1842
Portland, ME 04104
Phone: 207-873-0068
Fax: 207-873-0118
Website: www.financiallit.org

Internal Revenue Service (IRS)

1111 Constitution Ave., N.W.
Washington, DC 20224
Website: www.irs.gov

Iowa State University Extension and Outreach

2150 Beardshear Hall
Ames, IA 50011-2031
Toll-Free: 800-262-3804
Website: www.extension.iastate.edu

JA Worldwide

One Lincoln St.
24th Fl.
Boston, MA 02111
Phone: 617-315-8563
Website: www.jaworldwide.org

Jump$tart Coalition for Personal Financial Literacy

1001 Connecticut Ave., N.W., Ste. 640
Washington, DC 20036
Phone: 202-846-6780
Website: www.jumpstart.org
E-mail: info@jumpstart.org

Junior Achievement USA®

1 Education Way
Colorado Springs, CO 80906
Phone: 719-540-8000
Website: www.juniorachievement.org
E-mail: newmedia@ja.org

The Kiplinger Washington Editors, Inc.

1100 13th St., N.W., Ste. 1000
Washington, DC 20005
Toll-Free: 800-544-0155
Phone: 202-887-6400
Website: www.kiplinger.com
E-mail: sub.services@kiplinger.com

Morningstar, Inc.

22 W. Washington St.
Chicago, IL 60602
Phone: 312-384-4000
Website: www.morningstar.com
E-mail: productinfo@morningstar.com

The Motley Fool

2000 Duke St.
2nd Fl.
Alexandria, VA 22314
Phone: 703-838-3665
Fax: 703-254-1999
Website: www.fool.com

Mymoney.gov

1500 Pennsylvania Ave., N.W.
Washington, DC 20220
Toll-Free: 800-FED-INFO (800-333-4636)
Website: www.mymoney.gov

National Association of Personal Financial Advisors (NAPFA)

8700 W. Bryn Mawr Ave., Ste. 700N
Chicago, IL 60631
Toll-Free: 888-FEE-ONLY (888-333-6659)
Phone: 847-483-5400
Website: www.napfa.org
E-mail: info@napfa.org

National Endowment for Financial Education (NEFE)

1550 Market St., Ste. 475
Denver, CO 80202
Phone: 303-741-6333
Website: www.nefe.org

National Institute of Food and Agriculture (NIFA)

12th St., S.W., Jefferson Dr.
305-A Whitten Bldg.
Washington, DC 20250
Phone: 202-720-2791 (hotline)
Website: nifa.usda.gov
E-mail: nifa@usda.gov

Native Financial Education Coalition (NFEC)

1516 P St., N.W.
Washington, DC 20005
Phone: 202-466-7767
Website: www.nfec.us
E-mail: nfec@ncai.org

Operation HOPE, Inc.

226 Peachtree St., S.W.
Atlanta, GA 30303
Website: www.operationhope.org

Plan Sponsor Council of America (PSCA)

4401 N. Fairfax Dr., Ste. 600
Arlington, VA 22203
Phone: 703-516-9300
Fax: 703-516-9303
Website: www.psca.org
E-mail: customercare@psca.org

Practical Money Skills

900 Metro Center Blvd.
Foster City, CA 94404-2172
Website: www.practicalmoneyskills.com
E-mail: info@practicalmoneyskills.com

Securities Industry and Financial Markets Association (SIFMA)

120 Bdwy., 35th Fl.
New York, NY 10271
Phone: 212-313-1200
Website: www.sifma.org

Society of Financial Service Professionals (FSP)

10 E. Athens Ave., Ste. 224
Ardmore, PA 19003
Toll-Free: 800-392-6900
Phone: 610-526-2500
Website: national.societyoffsp.org

TreasuryDirect KIDS

Website: www.treasurydirect.gov/kids/kids.htm

U.S. Securities and Exchange Commission (SEC)

100 F St., N.E.
Washington, DC 20549
Website: www.sec.gov

USAA Educational Foundation (USAAEF)

9800 Fredericksburg Rd.
San Antonio, TX 78288-0026
Website: www.usaaef.org
E-mail: edfoundation_info@usaa.com

Consumer Information and Insurance

American Consumer Credit Counseling (ACCC)

130 Rumford Ave., Ste. 202
Auburndale, MA 02466-1371
Toll-Free: 800-769-3571
Phone: 617-559-5700
Fax: 617-244-1116
Website: www.consumercredit.com
E-mail: info@consumercredit.com

American Council of Life Insurers (ACLI)

101 Constitution Ave., N.W., Ste. 700
Washington, DC 20001-2133
Toll-Free: 877-674-4659
Phone: 202-624-2000
Website: www.acli.com
E-mail: contact@acli.com

Consumer Action

57 Post St., Ste. 611
San Francisco, CA 94104
Phone: 415-777-9635
Fax: 415-777-5267
Website: www.consumer-action.org
E-mail: info@consumer-action.org

Consumer Checkbook

1625 K St., N.W.
8th Fl.
Washington, DC 20006
Toll-Free: 800-213-7283
Website: www.checkbook.org
E-mail: support@checkbook.org

Consumer Federation of America (CFA)
1620 I St., N.W., Ste. 200
Washington, DC 20006
Phone: 202-387-6121
Website: www.consumerfed.org
E-mail: cfa@consumerfed.org

Consumer Financial Protection Bureau (CFPB)
P.O. Box 2900
Clinton, IA 52733-2900
Toll-Free: 855-411-2372
Toll-Free TTY: 855-729-2372
Website: www.consumerfinance.gov

Consumer Reports Online
101 Truman Ave.
Yonkers, NY 10703
Toll-Free: 800-333-0663
Website: www.consumerreports.org

Consumer World
Shore Dr.
Somerville, MA 02145
Website: www.consumerworld.org

Insurance Information Institute (III)
110 William St.
New York, NY 10038
Phone: 212-346-5500
Website: www.iii.org
E-mail: info@iii.org

Kids' Finance
P.O. Box 241775
Los Angeles, CA 90024
Website: www.kidsfinance.com
E-mail: contact@kidsfinance.com

National Consumer Law Center, Inc. (NCLC)

7 Winthrop Sq.
Boston, MA 02110-1245
Phone: 617-542-8010
Fax: 617-542-8028
Website: www.nclc.org
E-mail: consumerlaw@nclc.org

National Consumers League (NCL)

1701 K St., N.W., Ste. 1200
Washington, DC 20006
Phone: 202-835-3323
Fax: 202-835-0747
Website: www.nclnet.org
E-mail: info@nclnet.org

Credit Reporting and Credit Scoring Agencies and Information

Credit Union National Association (CUNA)

99 M St., S.E., Ste. 300
Washington, DC 20003
Toll-Free: 800-356-9655
Website: www.cuna.org
E-mail: hello@cuna.coop

Credit.org

1450 Iowa Ave., Ste. 200
Riverside, CA 92507
Toll-Free: 800-431-8157
Phone: 951-414-2454
Website: www.credit.org

Equifax, Inc.

P.O. Box 740241
Atlanta, GA 30374
Toll-Free: 888-202-4025
Website: www.equifax.com

Experian Information Solutions, Inc.

475 Anton Blvd.
Costa Mesa, CA 92626
Phone: 714-830-7000
Website: www.experian.com

National Credit Union Administration (NCUA)

1775 Duke St.
Alexandria, VA 22314
Phone: 703-518-6300
Website: www.ncua.gov

PIA (National Association of Professional Insurance Agents)

419 N. Lee St.
Alexandria, VA 22314
Phone: 703-836-9340
Fax: 703-836-1279
Website: www.pianet.org
E-mail: web@pianet.org

TransUnion LLC

2 Baldwin Pl.
P.O. Box 1000
Chester, PA 19016
Toll-Free: 800-888-4213
Website: www.transunion.com

Information about Debt Management, Collection Practices, and Bankruptcy

ACA International

3200 Courthouse Ln.
Eagan, MN 55121-1585
Toll-Free: 800-269-1607
Website: www.acainternational.org

Consolidated Credit, Inc.

5701 W. Sunrise Blvd.
Fort Lauderdale, FL 33313
Toll-Free: 800-320-9929
Website: www.consolidatedcredit.org
E-mail: Counselor@ConsolidatedCredit.org

CuraDebt Systems, LLC.

4000 Hollywood Blvd., Ste. 555-S
Hollywood, FL 33021
Toll-Free: 877-850-3328
Phone: 754-333-5506
Fax: 754-333-5510
Website: www.curadebt.com
E-mail: counselors@curadebt.com

National Foundation for Credit Counseling (NFCC)

2000 M St., N.W., Ste. 505
Washington, DC 20036
Toll-Free: 800-388-2227
Phone: 202-677-4300
Website: espanol.nfcc.org

Navient Solutions, Inc.

P.O. Box 9500
Wilkes-Barre, PA 18773-9500
Toll-Free: 800-428-1039
Website: www.navient.com
E-mail: nvoptout@navient.com

CHAPTER 48

MOBILE APPS FOR FINANCIAL MANAGEMENT

Omnigraphics is not liable for any damages arising from the use of or inability to use the listed apps or any services contained in it, or from any action or decision taken as a result of using the listed apps. The inclusion of an application does not imply that Omnigraphics endorses or has approved the mentioned applications.

App Name	Features	Free/Paid	Website
Cash App	• Send and receive money • Buy, sell, deposit, and withdraw Bitcoins • Buy and sell stocks	Free	www.cash.app
Debt Payoff Planner	• Track all your loans in one place • Get customized debt repayment plans and schedule	Free	www.debt-payoff-planner.com/
Expensify	• Track expenses • Scan receipts • Track and submit receipts	Free/In-App Purchases	www.expensify.com
FreshBooks	• Navigate the stock market • Compare and evaluate stocks • Track the performance of your portfolio	Free/In-App Purchases	www.freshbooks.com
Google Pay	• Pay bills • Send and receive money • Track expenses and savings	Free	pay.google.com
Mint	• Monitor transactions, expenses, and subscriptions • Track IRS tax refunds • Set and manage financial goals • Get tips to spend smarter and save money • Get credit score and credit report	Free/In-App Purchases	www.mint.intuit.com

App Name	Features	Free/Paid	Website
PayPal	• Send and receive money • Scan and pay • Split and pay bills • Buy, sell, and hold cryptocurrency (only in U.S. and limited in certain states)	Free	www.paypal.com
QuickBooks Online Mobile	• Manage your business • Manage cash flow • Create, send, and track invoices • Track sales	Paid	www.quickbooks.intuit.com
SigFig Wealth Management	• Monitor your investments • Manage your portfolio • Get access to licensed advisors	Free	www.sigfig.com
Stripe	• Keep track of your business • Compare historical business data • Maintain customer and transaction data • Issue refunds	Free	www.stripe.com
Tally	• Manage your debts • Get debt payoff strategies • Organize your cards	Free	www.meettally.com
Toshl Finance	• Connect with bank and credit cards • Monitor expenses • Budgeting	Free/In-App Purchases	www.toshl.com
Venmo	• Send and receive money • Manage money • Shop online • Shop using Venmo debit card • Pay in stores using QR code • Create a business profile and sell products	Free	www.venmo.com
Yahoo Finance	• Navigate the stock market • Compare and evaluate stocks • Track the performance of your portfolio	Free/In-App Purchases	www.finance.yahoo.com
Zelle®	• Send money and receive money • Move money directly from bank account to bank account	Free	www.zellepay.com

INDEX

INDEX

Page numbers that appear in *Italics* refer to tables or illustrations. Page numbers that have a small 'n' after the page number refer to citation information shown as Notes. Page numbers that appear in **Bold** refer to information contained in boxes within the chapters.

C

D

E

F

G

K

L

M

N

O

P

Q

R

S

T

U

V

W

Y

Z